GOD

LEFT FOOTPRINTS

ON MY

HEART

stories Worth sharing

James Matthew Rioux

ISBN 979-8-88851-686-7 (Paperback)
ISBN 979-8-88851-687-4 (Digital)

Covenant Books
11661 Hwy 707
Murrells Inlet, SC 29576
www.covenantbooks.com

God has to get us to where He wants us to be so we can see what He wants us to see.

—Pastor Shedrick Winfield

FOREWORD

By Greg Dykstra, PhD

In the past, older generations passed their experiences onto their children and grandchildren by storytelling around a campfire.

James has revived that custom for us by placing a fire in the heart of the reader. He is a storyteller of high rank. James references another storyteller, Habakkuk. This biblical prophet's message was that even if he lost everything, he would rejoice in the God Who strengthens him in hard times.

"Yet I will rejoice in the LORD, I will take joy in the God of my salvation" (Habakkuk 3:18 ESV).

James rejoices by referencing God's grace in challenging life situations. He expresses radical trust and engages the reader in such a way that, despite tears moistening your cheeks, you will hesitate to wipe them away.

"Set a spell" and enjoy messages from his heart to his descendants. He has lived a life worthy of sharing.

PREFACE

I suppose that the real genesis of this book of true stories, unbeknownst to me at the time, has its beginning in 2012 as I watched a movie that I reference in "Table First." The reader will soon notice the thread that weaves its way throughout these pages—being that God is not a random God and that He gives each of us spiritual gifts that He fully intends to call into service within the course of our lives.

The movie is a true story about a marine that had taken a stateside post after having served a stint during Desert Storm in Iraq after the conflict intensified. He then volunteers to escort the body of Chance Phelps, a soldier from his former unit, back to his home in the United States. The scene that was forever impressed upon my mind takes place at the VFW hall in the young man's hometown shortly after their arrival.

The following is the dialogue between the marine escort and an older veteran sitting at the bar:

> Lt. Col. Mike Strobl. I stayed home. I was trained to fight. If I'm not over there, what am I? Those guys, guys like Chance... they're Marines.
>
> Charlie Fitts. And you think you're not? Want to be with your family every night—you think you have to justify that? You'd better stop right there, sir. You've brought Chance home. You're his witness now. Without a witness, they just disappear.

This exchange, though much more dramatic than anything that I can offer here, is at the very core of the message that I have stitched throughout these stories.

The message that lies herein is that each of us must share the stories of our life using the gifts that God has given us. If we do not tell them with our unique perspective, they just die, just as Charlie Fitts so eloquently expressed.

It does not get any more complicated than that. Tell your stories!

And please do not attempt this on your own. Call upon God as it is written in James 1:5.

*The most powerful person in the world
is the storyteller. The storyteller sets
the vision, values, and agenda of an
entire generation that is to come.*

—Steve Jobs

INTRODUCTION

I have always imagined myself as a motivational speaker, on stages around the world, whipping an audience into a frenzy as I waxed eloquently on whatever the occasion called for. But the problem with imagination is that, well, it is all in my imagination. What I knew deep down was that I was a writer. And God knew! He had plans for my writing. As I was collecting my thoughts after "the call," which started me beating the bushes for a structure for this book, I was soon made to realize that God had caused me to be a witness to many unique and remarkable events in my life.

(Warning: First warning, the first story is already here. Second warning, I use run-on sentences.)

I am a truck driver, so how about a unique and amazing story?

Many years ago, I picked up a load of seawater from the Gulf of Mexico on the coast of south Louisiana. Destination? It was going all the way to Dartmouth, Nova Scotia, right on the coast of the Atlantic Ocean, for a crazy reason. This seawater was going to the Mobil docks for use in the offshore oil drilling industry. It seemed that they used the water to keep the drill bits cool in the grinding and drilling process. I was told that the water from the Gulf of Mexico had a much higher salt content than the water in the North Atlantic Ocean. Because of that, it added benefit to the grinding and drilling process that was worth the additional shipping costs. Now that you know why I brought sea water 3,600 miles from one ocean to another, I can continue.

The time of this trip is easy to remember because I just happened to be taking the interstate loop around Boston, Massachusetts, on the evening of July 4, 2001, after returning to the United States from Canada. My parents loved to listen to the Boston Pops featuring Arthur Fiedler and The Boston Symphony Orchestra. This was the Fourth of July, which meant their iconic Independence Day program would be broadcast, and well, I was near Boston and was trying to find the program on the radio. I never found it on the AM or FM channels in these pre-live-streaming days.

The other thing that I could not find were American flags on display on this July 4 holiday. There was an almost spooky absence of them everywhere I looked. Geez, I had just driven through Lexington, Massachusetts, where Paul Revere was summoned for his midnight ride to warn the colonists of approaching British troops in 1775. Less than fifteen miles away was Boston Harbor, where there had been a little party of sorts two years earlier in protest of the Tea Act of 1773. Boston is considered to be the birthplace of American freedom, and a few miles south of Boston is New Bedford, the birthplace of my father.

By comparison, I had just returned from Canada on Sunday, July 1, as they were celebrating Canada Day, their Fourth of July–like holiday. The Canadian maple leaf flag was displayed everywhere, hanging on buildings, cars, everywhere, you name it—but not in America. What was wrong with Americans? Where were their patriotism and pride? They fly their favorite NFL football and college team flags and put bumper stickers everywhere. Old Glory was hauntingly absent. So where were all the flags?

But then, a little more than two months later, the 911 attack on America occurred, and suddenly, with this outrageous act of violence on our soil, flags sprung up everywhere, on buildings, with little plastic rods placed on car doors, everywhere. My country, which was not proud enough to fly the red, white, and blue just two months prior, now could not run one up the flagpole fast enough, with flag makers throughout America unable to meet demand for Betsy Ross's pride and joy.

But just three months later, as a truck driver, I saw something that sickened me. Those same American flags that had adorned just about every car on the US highways after 911 were now littering the highways, "from the mountains to the prairies to the oceans."

I realized that God had given me this incredibly unique perspective, one that few people had the opportunity to witness and then to also make the connection. This was only brought about because of my trip to these two countries during these exclusive dates. Why me? Who was I to be a witness and a participant in this and so many other unique circumstances?

I liked to write and began using social media early during its infancy as a communication tool. Unbeknownst to me, God was using this new venue as my practice field of sorts, prompting me to record my thoughts on Facebook posts to gauge my abilities and engage my little audience of friends. Some of my posts resulted in incredibly positive responses from my followers.

Encouraged by the comments, including one post that went viral (kind of), I started submitting the occasional article to a local newspaper, and to my surprise, some of my submissions were published in a section for "Wannabe Writers." Though I was not paid for my efforts when they were published, the excitement of seeing my words in a publication was exhilarating.

I vividly remember one of the first ones being printed on a particular Sunday in 2012 about a subject matter about which I write in the first chapter of this book. As the pride of having my first article printed and having my vision enlarged, all I could see back then were the mistakes, improper sentence structure, and incongruous ideas that I thought originally were well connected. Nevertheless, I was thinking that I wanted to make sure that the protagonist in my first published article was aware of it. So the next morning, after it was published, I called her at her office, and it went something like this:

Me. Mona Collins? This is James Rioux. I was at your office a few weeks ago, and well, I had written an article for the paper about my experience, and it was published in the paper yesterday. I just wanted to make sure that you saw it.

Mona. Mr. Rioux! Yes, I saw it! *She screamed into the phone,* I had to leave church because my phone was exploding. I thought somebody had died in my family. Everyone was asking me if I had seen the article. What article, and what does that have to do with me? I am in church for goodness' sake.

Having read it after being forced to leave Sunday Mass, she then explained that she did remember that a photographer from the paper had come by earlier in the week to take pictures of her. She then had to tell him that he could not just stroll into her office and start snapping away. There were privacy and legal issues to deal with concerning something of that nature.

PHOTOGRAPHER. But, Mona, a man wrote an amazing article about you and the work of your office.

Mona then thanked me for the beautiful article. However, it was just a little after 8:00 a.m. at this point and it was at that exact moment that neither one of us had even an inkling of the series of events that a simple and humble submission in a local newspaper would precipitate in our lives. We would not see or speak to each other for six years.

An amazing article? Really? Me? Naw, this ain't happening, I thought to myself at the time.

"An amazing article," the photographer told Ms. Mona. To this day, my mind still cannot process that combination of words being hurled my way. In fact, I still get emotional eleven years later and cannot finish without choking up when telling that story. That story, "THAT STORY."

I remembered for years that friends and acquaintances had randomly related to me that one of the things they liked about me the most is my storytelling. Once, not too long ago, I went to the funeral home to pay my respects to a friend from high school who had lost a daughter at a much too young of an age.

One of the many friends whom I had not seen for many years was weaving his way through this packed funeral parlor and walked up to me just to say that he loves looking at Facebook every morning to see my stories. He said he is always uplifted in some way because of my writing. He thanked me. I expressed my appreciation for his kind words, but I thought to myself, *Geez, that's a lot of weaving and bobbing just to tell an old broken-down truck driver that he liked my posts.*

Wait a minute, do my stories have a fan base? No, not ole Jim Bob. Again, I do not process compliments very well. I now know why, but heretofore, it has stopped me for too many years from even considering a sincere effort to put all these stories or anything else into book form, as many had suggested to me. But God's timing is not ours, nor are our plans always in line with His plans for our spiritual gifts.

Truth be known, there has always been a family member who has been overly critical of me and my every utterance. He would just look at me sometimes and say, "Shut up, Jim." And for all these years, I shut up. I have allowed him to "live rent-free in my head" for years, to coin an original phrase. My spiritual gifts and creative DNA have been emotionally paralyzed for most of my adult life because of this.

"But as for you, ye thought evil against me, but God meant it unto good, to bring to pass, as it is this day" (Genesis 50:20 KJV).

I must admit to myself that I allowed it; it is said that someone cannot inflict such a condition upon us without our permission.

However, two recent conversations occurred that were to become the kindling of the fire required to ignite the writing of this book; neither were onetime events.

My grandson Luke? The dude loves football. When he was about thirteen years old, I brought him and his brother Owen to a New Orleans Saints football preseason training camp. That day's team activities included field goal practice where the ball was kicked through uprights placed along the sidelines in front of the crowd-filled stands. This was done as an interactive exercise for the spectators where several kicks go into the crowd of men as was intended. However, most of the men could not handle the catch and dropped the ball.

On one kick though, I hollered, "Coming your way, Luke." This football dude of ours just nonchalantly reached up and gathered the ball in his waiting arms. No problem here, folks. The crowd of men gave this thirteen-year-old teenager a roaring and standing ovation. Proud Paw Paw moment for sure!

On another occasion later in the day, as I had been trying to keep track of the two boys, I could not find Luke. I nervously asked his younger brother, "Where is Luke?"

"He's down there," Owen replied.

I looked toward the area to which he pointed and asked again, "Where?"

Again, but this time a little aggravated, Owen replied, "Paw Paw, you see that big circle of men down there? Luke is right in the middle of them."

Then a little worried, I casually eased down the stands toward this testosterone-filled bunch so as not to catch Luke's attention. As I listened in on the conversation, these men, one after another, were asking my young grandson about statistics and other info concerning each of the players on the field. In rapid-fire succession, he answered each question quickly and confidently, even correcting one or two of them with what they thought they knew about the player.

As I gingerly climbed back up, I anxiously called my daughter, his mother. "Jessica," I screamed into the phone. "Who is this kid?"

After she had calmed me down and inquired as to which "kid" I was referring to, she said, "Daddy, Luke's research of player stats, that is all he does. He loves his football."

Now let's talk about that first conversation that helped me write seriously. Luke, who is graduating from high school as of this writing, has been offered scholastic scholarships but has also played high school football at defensive end. On several occasions, especially after a game in which he did exceptionally well with several tackles and quarterback sacks, his mother and I would walk down to the field, and this brief exchange would occur:

ME. Luke, that was a heck of a game you had tonight.

LUKE. *Answering without a second of hesitation*, But, Paw Paw, I'm too small to play football.

The context at the time was that someone—and I certainly hoped it was not me—had told him that he was not big enough to play football. Now he could have whined the rest of his life about how someone demeaned and offended him, causing him not to pursue his own dream.

Well, now it seems that his Paw Paw has done exactly that same thing concerning his potential for writing. Not Luke; he used that criticism as his energy pill and a 24-7 locker-room motivation speech, on and off the field. In fact, it had worked so well that there was at least one time when the coach pulled him from the game for one play just to calm him down because he was *really* in his zone. The results? Team captain, all-district honors, and his school's defensive MVP. Yes, that kid, the football dude.

The icing on the cake is that I recently asked him who told him he was too small to play football.

His startling response? "Probably me, Paw Paw!"

My takeaway was that this little phrase was his way of pumping himself up, and it worked. As of this writing, he is now attending his first semester at Louisiana State University. He is one of seven thousand first-year students with a total student enrollment of thirty-five thousand; he will need all the motivation he can get. It is a small-fish-in-a-big-pond story. In his case, he went from being the big fish in a small pond, and that transition was not easy.

"But, Paw Paw, I'm too small to play football."

God would not allow those words to stop ringing in my ears. We, as parents and grandparents, are supposed to wear the hats of motivators and teachers. Sometimes, as we take the time to obey the "still, small voice," our children and grandchildren will teach us about perseverance in our own lives concerning many things that they know nothing about.

The second attitude-adjusting conversation was not a conversation at all, for that would have required two active participants. This was a "shut up and listen, Daddy" moment to which I quickly obeyed and am forever grateful.

For five years, my daughter Jessica had been telling me that I should write a book. The subject matter always escaped me, though. I have never been a man of few spoken words—to a fault, just ask my family. One member told me that I was "so random," with me not knowing whether that was a compliment or criticism. My dad always had to quiet me down and told me that I spoke as if I were in a sawmill, loudly.

And then about two years later, Jessica returned from a church-women's conference with a gift for me. It was a book about Habakkuk from the Old Testament. I was raised in a church that had not talked too much about the Bible or even encouraged the flock to make reading it a daily habit. I was not that familiar with the Old Testament, just the four gospels in the New Testament. One of my pastors told me that I did not need to read the Bible but just listen to his sermons on Sunday. I was never made to realize just how outlandish that statement was until many years later.

With the book in hand and what surely was a confused look on my face, I thanked Jessica and asked her about the conference, her noting that I was changing the subject, to which she replied, "Daddy, Habakkuk was a scribe. He was a writer. He wrote of the things that God made him a witness of."

Okay, I saw where this was going.

"Daddy, you are a writer. You have a gift that has touched lives. You are our family scribe."

And I left. I read the book and could not put it down, which is unusual for me. It intrigued me. I began feeling and seeing a purpose in my writing about the things that God had made me a witness to. I began thinking about the family members who told me that I was random and about the things that I had witnessed throughout my life. Surely, I had written about some of them in a local newspaper. I then began to see that they did not just occur randomly at all. I started to make connections. At this moment, with the Habakkuk book still on my nightstand, a gentle, meandering personal vision of a book started creeping in.

But that was three years ago, and I still had not seriously considered beginning the process. For most of those five years, I was pondering who I was and what I honestly believed on a myriad of topics. But something of the nature of a real live book had to have a clear and concise conceptual structure, a purpose. And somehow, by some heavenly power, I had to evict this critical voice in my head that repeatedly said to me, "You are not an author. You are a truck driver. Truck drivers do not write books." I believed him. Even if the voice wasn't real, it was greatly exaggerated.

Then "the call" I mentioned occurred very unexpectedly—

The caller ID was my daughter Jessica. "Daddy, it is time to start writing!" she screamed into the phone. "Shelve the nutrition and life-coaching business and start writing. Daddy, you are a scribe, a storyteller. Daddy, evict that hateful voice from your head immediately and take away his key. Daddy, it is time to start writing."

And the words she said that will never be forgotten were, "I do not want something to happen to you without your grandchildren being able to read your stories. You have a gift, so be obedient and start writing." Then she abruptly ended the call.

I had to force a huge emotional lump back down my throat. I had not said anything but hello. She was right. God was right. It was time. I looked down. The "call ended" still stared back up from the phone at me. I did not even have a chance to stutter.

I heard what she screamed through the phone that day. It was a Friday. But for what seemed like the hundredth time in my life, someone told me, "It's your stories." At that time, it was communicated to me at decibels much higher than the one in the funeral home. It was said to me forcefully yet poignantly, but above everything else, I heard the word *stories*.

This time, *stories* had been uttered by someone who loved me and whose opinion I valued greatly. She is a single mom whose very visible struggles have caused many immensely powerful lessons to be instilled in her children.

Her pastor refers to her as "prophetic." Each generation or so, a family is blessed with one. She has called me a scribe, the family scribe, and each family has one of those also.

I am a writer, and the most creative and fulfilling moments of my life have sprung up in the early morning hours, during my quiet time. I call it my prime time, when I feel God's presence the strongest. It is at these moments that He speaks to me in soft pastels instead of the harsh tones that He may have to use later in the day. It is during these predawn hours that I text my thoughts which I feel I must record in some form so that they may be preserved, at least for me. In many cases, those brief notes were transformed into a text to my daughters, a Facebook post, and sometimes a submission to the local paper for publishing consideration. Then rarely, they were published. In the chapters to follow, I write of two such newspaper submissions upon which the idea for this book was formed.

I am a storyteller. Yes, I am. And in this moment of declaration, I screamed like my daughter screamed at me, "I am a storyteller. I am a writer." If my story touches one person or makes someone smile on a difficult day or if it changes a life, well, that is my reward.

As the reader absorbs each of the stories that follow, I do ask you to not focus so much on the writer but on the exquisite timing and effort that God expends in creating a vortex that joins two or more people together in the same moment and place and, in many cases, creates a forever moment.

These moments are like an artist creating a beautiful tapestry about our life. As it is being stitched together, we do not see it for what it will become, for we are seeing it from the back as just a bunch of unconnected threads. But God knows.

May I encourage you to wait on Him, and He will make it known unto you. We are not capable of seeing His finished work of art in advance. But do learn for yourself that there is also power and beauty in blind obedience.

God always knows the end from the beginning. He knows who we are, what we are capable of, and the plans He has for our spiritual gifts. He also knows how these exquisitely timed events will affect the lives of others if we are obedient and tell the story. As many others have stated in other places, our spiritual gifts are given by God, and we are entrusted with them, and we must give them away.

To know of God's majesty is to be made aware of His love for each of us as manifested in episodes like those that follow in the upcoming stories. In fact, as this storyteller commences his offerings, please note that in this introduction, many of his stories are there. Go figure!

As you read, I invite you to jot down comparable stories from your life that could brighten someone's day or inspire a young person to rise above their adversity. Your story could very well inspire a cloistered, aging, unknown, writer, and truck driver who thinks that their time has long since passed.

It could happen!

Tell the story!

"Paw Paw, I'm not big enough to play football."

"Rioux, it's your stories."
"Daddy, start writing."
And then, there was a still, small voice.

A CONCLUSION AND A BEGINNING

I now had something concrete to work with, and with tears in my eyes (some truck drivers do cry), I searched a few Christian book publishers and found Ashley, who seemed as excited as me. Moving forward, as I fired up the laptop out on the road in truck stops at night when I could, the words just flowed as I pecked away on the keyboard at a less-than-warp speed.

This was happening!

At last!

(Cue: "At Last" by Etta James, "I found a dream that I could speak to, a dream that I can call my own, I found a thrill to rest my cheek to, a thrill that I had never known…For you are mine, at last.")

Since one of the catalysts for this book was Habakkuk, the chapters will be marked as "Tables" as referred to in Habakkuk 2:2, which reads, "Write the vision and make it plain upon the tables." While the actual meaning and context of *tables* in the text could have various meanings, "chapters" just did not seem right for this book.

The first few *tables* will be based on some of my published stories, especially the ones from which I received feedback. I would pray that this offering is constructed in such a manner that you would not feel compelled to read it straight through but that you would return to it and read them repeatedly for your own inspiration, as I was inspired to write them. My prayer is that this book will inspire others to force their memories out of an abandoned file somewhere in their past to be shared with their grandchildren. I do advise that you jot these memories down immediately as they come, for they are fleeting and will crawl back to where they emanated, not to return on command.

At last, I am writing. Thanks, Jessica, and even the critical family member. Also, thanks to all those who tolerated my stories down through the years and to those who loved them. At last, my stories will have a fan base that can read them for years and decades to come.

Especially thanks to my grandchildren; hence, I conclude each table with, "Much love, Paw Paw."

Herein lies my stories.

Enjoy!

Much love,
—Paw Paw

I will stand upon my watch and set me
upon the tower and will watch to see
what He will say unto me and what I shall
answer when I am reproved.

And the Lord answered me and said
"Write the vision and make it plain upon
tables, that he may run that readeth it.

For the vision is yet for an appointed
time, but at the end it shall speak and
not lie; though it tarry, wait for it; because
it will surely come, it will not tarry.

—Habakkuk 2:1–3

FIRST TABLE

Jury Duty

"James Matthew Rioux, you are hereby commanded to appear for jury duty at the Nineteenth Judicial District Court building." Blah, blah, blah! Whoa, wait a minute. This was not gonna happen. The twelve-dollar-a-day pay for jury duty would break my less-than-stable bank account in a matter of hours.

Who do I contact? There it is: one Mona Gills-Collins, jury coordinator. A very terse but short "this ain't gonna happen" letter was written and addressed to said Ms. Mona. *Whew, I'm glad I caught that in time. That's taken care of.* And I waited and waited until the Friday before the Monday that I had been "commanded to appear" and still had not received a reply. I got this Mona, a public servant, on the phone and asked her where my excused absence reply was.

Then her terse but short reply was, "Request denied, Mr. Rioux. See you on Monday." A "call ended" was staring me in the face—again, and again, there was no time to stutter. My financial future was collapsing before my very eyes. I then quickly placed a call to my boss to tell him that my carefully worded "this ain't going to happen" request was vehemently denied. The very loud sucking noise of any kind of financial stability in my life had been foremost in my thoughts.

Monday morning, parking garage, long walk, metal detectors, lengthy line, a big blank wall that seemed like a detention area, which was to be my confined space for a few minutes—I checked in and

1

took a seat in the big room, with many seats soon to be filled with many people. I wondered, *What bill I wouldn't be able to pay next week because of this interruption to my illustrious trucking career?*

Then she appeared at the podium, one Mona Gills-Collins, the request denier. *There she is in all her glory*, I thought to myself. *Why is this happening to me?*

Well, Jim Bob, you are here. Time to listen up and find a loophole in all this info we are being given.

As I stated previously, God has a long-standing process of placing us in situations and around people who, at the time, may seem like adversity in its purest form. As we go forward, please remember how Habakkuk was told by the Lord to just write the vision—or rather, his witness—of the events that he was instructed to witness. Habakkuk even got a little testy with God, but he was soon told that the purpose of his writing was for a time yet to come.

Well, as Ms. Mona was taking us through this seemingly senseless drudgery, I certainly was not thinking about Habakkuk of the Old Testament—maybe Moses waiting for the Red Sea to part—but that did not seem to be in my future anytime soon with Cruella de Vil in charge. Even the story of Job came to mind, but I digress.

Her next bit of torture was a very sterile, government-issued video on jury duty and our patriotic responsibility. Okay, I must admit that I felt a little, an ever so slight, almost imperceptible twitch that began the underlying process of bringing me on board this soon to be runaway train of civic duty, but don't let me get ahead of myself.

Next up was Judge Wilson Fields who got us laughing about a variety of things. But what was amazing about him was his ability to talk to a complete stranger, and after a very few minutes, after asking seemingly unrelated questions, he could correctly guess a person's occupation. After a couple of demonstrations, this distraction calmed the group down a bit. Okay, it calmed me down.

The time to let the computer start selecting potential jurors at random came. Mona started calling a few names and then leading them to the courtroom upstairs for the next phase of the jury selection process. She then started a movie to keep us occupied and distracted.

But it was not just any movie; "the movie" would not only get my pendulum of patriotic duty swinging to Mona's side but also—this movie that I had not even heard of—would forever change my life, especially on holidays like Veterans Day, the Fourth of July, and Memorial Day. It would bring to mind Ray Charles singing "America the Beautiful."

She had put in the movie *Taking Chance* with Kevin Bacon, who played the part of a marine lieutenant colonel who escorts the body of a soldier killed on active duty. With little dialogue and very emotional scenes of various kinds, such as entire airports coming to a complete stop as the casket was being loaded from one vehicle and plane to another, this movie painted a very moving illustration of the entire process of bringing a soldier home with exquisitely created imagery. Well-deserved shame on my part began to ooze from somewhere.

The movie had its intended effect. "Touché. Ms. Mona, although you have done an excellent job of making me a seeming convert to this cause, you haven't finished me off yet."

"Little did I know" does not begin to describe the ace up her sleeve that she was about to throw down like a royal flush. But what was to come was an exchange between her and me that she was prepared for, obviously. As Monday was dragged into Tuesday and then another day, in desperation, at some point on Wednesday, I walked up to the counter behind where she stood, and now almost desperate, I tossed the following words in her direction: "Mona, you have no idea what this week will do to me financially if it continues."

She responded without a nanosecond of hesitation, "Mr. Rioux, it is not possible this week for you to sacrifice anything close to that of the men and women with their names on the wall outside."

My figurative white flag was flapping in the torrent created by the words that she hurled back at me so eloquently. All I could feel seething through my prefrontal cortex was, *Game, set, match!* Poke me with a fork. I was done. She had won!

Feelings of anger quickly morphed into shame at being so insensitive and self-centered. The feelings of obligation to public service in the greatest country on earth through jury duty had then been clearly established in my mind. And then, to heighten the sense of shame and humiliation that I had already inflicted upon myself, God placed another angel in my midst.

As I returned to the juror's waiting area after a break, I was looking around for a seat and found one a couple of places from the end of a row where a beautiful woman was seated. I took a seat close to her. And then, though not directed at me, I was able to hear her story. It was a testimony to me personally. I was made to understand the gravity of this moment, that week—all of it.

She was sitting in a wheelchair because of a carjacking that was perpetrated against her and her husband. In the commission of the crime, her husband was killed, and she was left permanently paralyzed. There was an opportunity after Mona's introductions and orientation that I had missed noticing in all my anger. Mona had called upon anyone who thought they could still wiggle their way out of all this to form a line and plead their case.

Despite that opportunity, there sat this beautiful lady, who could very well have taken that opportunity to be excused but refused. In her explanation to me and a few others sitting by her, she explained that she still thought it was her responsibility to fulfill her obligation to her community.

To further illustrate her commitment to moving on with her life without bitterness in the face of overwhelming adversity, God placed her in my midst a few years later at a rehabilitation hospital. I saw her approaching the door at the same time as my wife and me. After telling my wife that I recognized her from jury duty, I said hello, and I must have asked her if she was coming for an appointment. She replied instead that she performed service work for patients there who would benefit from an uplifting visit from volunteers like her.

The preceding story concerning my jury duty service in 2012 is an extended version of the one that I submitted to the local paper and that was then published.

One never knows who will read a published article, but in my situation, I had the clear and concise urge—an almost pleading of the spirit—to submit it. Having done so, just like the request sent to Mona to be excused from jury duty service, I had forgotten about it.

JURY DUTY 2.0

I did not know who or what Habakkuk was at the time the preceding jury duty service story was published. I had just been obedient to the spirit within that was telling me that someone would benefit from it, so it was submitted and published. And that is all I have ever done when writing on platforms like social media.

The "appointed time" came again six years later when I checked the mail and found another letter from the Nineteenth Judicial Court. Yes, you guessed it: "You are hereby commanded to appear…" It was signed by a familiar name, Mona Gills-Collins, and you know the rest. This time, though, there was no request for an excuse in the offing. I knew how that would end up. I would put on my best "It's great to be an American" game face and appear, as commanded, again!

It was the same routine as before—Monday morning, parking garage, long walk, metal detectors, long line by a big blank wall that seemed like a detention area that was to be my companion for a few minutes, waiting to be checked in. But hey, wait a minute. The big blank wall was not completely blank anymore. A few steps from the check-in counter hung a beautiful frame. I moved a little closer then, and I saw that someone had framed a newspaper article. Still, I moved a little closer, and I saw the writer's name: "James Matthew Rioux." There was my article from six years ago. *How did this happen? Who? Why? A truck driver whose critical family member was always telling him to shut up?*

I had been checked in. I sat in the "big room." My head was spinning. I sat through the introductions and orientation, still in a perplexed trance and still wondering. This time though, I had bothered myself to notice the instructions from Mona to line up in the "wiggle your way out of this" line, and the pleadings began. I waited for the line to die down and then lined up last. I checked to see that nobody was behind me, listening to the beggars wanting out, like me six years earlier. And then, Mona having reached the end of the line, asked, "Next?"

I humbly stepped up.

She very matter-of-factly asked, "How can I help you?"

I looked into her eyes, waiting for any hint of recognition from her—nothing.

She repeated a little louder, "How CAN I HELP YOU?"

The words, "Mona, do you remember me?" tumbled out of my mouth.

She very sarcastically replied, "No, HOW CAN I HELP YOU!"

"James Rioux," I replied.

She then twitched a little, cocked her head some, and paused.

I then pointed toward the wall by the check-in counter. "The newspaper article hanging on the wall outside."

"You're that James Rioux?" she quietly asked. "Can you meet me over there in about five minutes?"

I walked outside to the lobby where my article was, not knowing what was about to happen that would change the direction of my life. Arriving at the wall, I cannot swear to you that she put her arm through mine or held my hand, but maybe she did, and she began to speak, which is, to the best of my recollection, the following: "Mr. Rioux, let me tell you about that article. There are fifteen judges in this building, and more than half of them have that article hanging in their office." She then walked me over to the big plate glass windows overlooking North Boulevard. She then extended her arm and pointed to all the businesses lining the street. "Most of those businesses are involved in one way or another with this court, and I can bring you to several of them where your article hangs inside."

What could I say but "wow," and that could never begin to explain my shock. I mumbled something that was surely incoherent to her.

She then said, "But that's not the half of it." She led me back to the framed article on the formerly big, blank wall. "Mr. Rioux, you may never fully comprehend how that article changed my life."

As I was still speechless, she began to explain how much she loved her job but was about to quit six years ago because her boss was giving her a tough time beyond measure, and she could not take it anymore. In fact, the Friday before the Sunday that the article appeared in the paper, she told me that she had written her two-week notice that she would be handing in on Monday, the same Monday that I called to make sure she saw the article.

She decided to resign. But the article appeared, and then her phone exploded while she was at Sunday Mass.

"Mona, the article," each caller repeated.

"What article? I'm in church, for goodness' sake. What article, and what does that have to do with me?"

Then she recounted to me that the photographer from the local paper had taken pictures in the office the week before. She told the photographer that he couldn't just waltz in there and start snapping pictures and that there were privacy issues to consider.

The photographer told her, "But, Mona, a man wrote an amazing article."

Then at work that Monday, she received phone calls, texts, and visits from friends, lawyers, and judges—giving her an avalanche of congratulations on the article about her.

The two-week notice, in her purse, was not turned in. Because of the sheer weight and volume of the attention laid upon her by the article, like a cape deservingly placed upon the shoulders of a queen, her boss, the former jury coordinator, was the one who soon resigned. Mona received a promotion.

I later learned from Mona that it was not her who hung the article; it was a lawyer who surprised her by placing it in a beautiful frame.

Habakkuk 2:2–3 had struck again.

THE FRUITS OF OBEDIENCE

The following are my *what-if*s:

- What if Mona had excused me from jury duty?
- What if Mona had just put in a *Star Wars* movie instead?
- What if I had not made my final plea to Mona, having never heard her eloquent reply?
- What if I had never met the beautiful angel in the wheelchair?
- What if it had never occurred to me to write the article and submit it for publication?
- What if the paper had never published it?
- What if the paper did publish it just a week or month later?
- What if I had never been called back for jury duty the second time (which was in error because of a later discovered computer glitch that eliminated all registered voters under age thirty)?
- What if? What if? What if?

God's ways are not our ways, nor are His plans our plans. There are so many happenstances in this entire experience that could have occurred just a little differently or at another time that would have allowed Mona to quit her job or for the article to never have been written.

It does not require any more explanation on my part to point out God's hand in the everyday affairs of man as demonstrated in this one story.

Surrender to God's will. Obey His whisperings through the still, small voice. Identify your spiritual gifts. Find your quiet space and your prime time with God so that He may also speak to you in soft pastels instead of the harsher tones used during our hectic days.

And then write, dance, sing, paint, build, and speak.

And to God be the glory!

Much love,
—Paw Paw

Author with Mona Gills-Collins, Jury Coordinator, 19th Judicial District Court, Baton Rouge, Louisiana.

*There is no greater agony than bearing
an untold story inside of you.*

—Maya Angelou, American
poet (1928–2014)

SECOND TABLE

This Guy Loves You

The first time that I walked into Wally's Sunday school class, it was as if he always knew me. I would soon learn that he treated everyone like that. It would take me a while to realize that I had met him many years ago at scout meetings though those memories were very faint.

But there I was in a new church with my wife, and we did not know anyone. Wally had that way of making everyone feel comfortable and like a part of the family. His lessons were built around telling stories. He genuinely wanted the class to learn the subject matter.

I got to know him well each Sunday right there in that classroom, and it was in the same room that I pulled my first stunt on him, which created a bond between us.

Wally had this habit of after having explained a particular point very well. He would ask, "Is that not true?" For some reason, many folks ask that question in a quite common way: "Is that true?" But Wally loved to ask it the other way.

After a couple of Sundays, he came up to me after the lesson concluded and asked how I was enjoying the class. I took this opportunity to pull his leg a little. I told him that his teaching skills were exemplary, which they were, but that it would be nice if the class would answer his questions correctly. This was when I was introduced to his gruff side.

He bellowed back at me, "What do you mean?"

I replied, "Wally, you always ask, 'Is that not true?' The correct answer to the question asked that way should be no. When they answer yes to that question, they are agreeing that your point is, indeed, not true."

After having obviously used that question for many years, he said, "You're right." I obviously pulled his leg, but for the next few lessons, when he would make a point, he would pause, give me a glare, and then correctly ask the question, "Is that true?"

I had severely cramped his style, but a long-term bond had been forged. My wife, Mary, and I became close friends with him and his wife, Linda. She taught my wife the sport of full-contact garage sales. Getting the best stuff at the best price was not an activity to be taken lightly or for the timid. Those Saturday morning forays were the venue through which the two of them bonded.

The lessons from church continued on Sunday nights at their home, and we gathered with them and a few other friends and couples informally. This was just a weekly get-together that introduced us to other church members. Different couples took turns each Sunday night with a lesson of their choice, with most being interesting and informative. Some were designed as fun alternatives. At the conclusion of these gatherings, we were endeared by a long-standing tradition that when leaving their home, Wally would always say, "You know this guy loves you?" Then as we drove off, both he and his wife would give the hand sign "I love you" used by the hearing impaired.

Wally continued for many years to teach me one-on-one in his library as he would show me a book he was currently reading, always about scriptures or the history of the Christian church. He would make copies of things that he was reading online for me to read later. Sometimes I did, and sometimes I didn't if it was way over my head.

Many times, he would give me a book, and many times, I would take and read them. Sometimes I would give them right back and tell him, "Not yet." If there was one thing he loved to share, it was knowledge. He wanted to share with others the excitement of learning about the things he loved.

His shop was another center of instruction, showing me tools that I did not have a clue about. He took my son Travis under his wing and taught him one summer how to do things like wiring light fixtures. Because of his love for tools, he jokingly was not allowed to go to Harbor Freight by himself with a credit card or checkbook.

There were many things we did together, and some were just done separately by ourselves. Sometime around 2015, though, we started to lose him to the cruel condition of Alzheimer's. For me, I noticed how when he would lose his train of thought, he would just finish a sentence with the phrase, "what-cha-ma-call-it." It was not an uncommon thing for some people to say, but it was occurring increasingly more often for him, long enough for us to notice its increase in frequency.

Wally and I got into the habit of going on rides together in my pickup truck because it had satellite radio, and he discovered in Willie's Roadhouse, some incredibly old country music. One of our first little trips began during a visit when he told me that he wanted to go down the interstate a few miles near Satsuma, Louisiana, to see a navy fighter jet that was on display in a park just off the exit on the service road.

We left the ladies at the house, and we took off. Usually, when we would arrive at a destination, I would go around and help him out of the truck because he had difficulty sometimes because of an industrial accident he had many years prior, resulting in having two metal hips. But this time, though, he was stretching his neck as we approached the plane, and then he was out of the truck in a flash. He was like a kid at the candy store. He was so excited as he practically ran up to it and started petting it like a kitten, explaining what everything on the plane was used for in detail.

At some point, he turned around and saw the perplexed look on my face. He had earlier told me that he had been wanting to come down to see it but never had the chance.

He said, as an explanation, "Jim, you don't understand. I was in the navy for four years stuck in a radio room, but this is the closest I've ever been to one of these jets." A special moment in his life was made special in mine just by my witness, a forever memory.

The trips became a regular occurrence. Every time we would go to their house, Mary would barely have enough time to get out of the pickup before he would jump in, sometimes just wearing socks on his feet and sometimes barefoot.

He was not driving any longer, and his outside, unsupervised activities became limited because of his condition, so the trips were an opportunity for him to get out of the house and served to give his wife a break.

This man with Alzheimer's, who was already beginning to forget some family members' names, would get in the truck and tell me to put the radio on Willie's "wat-cha-ma-call-it," and then he would sing along, word for word, with songs that I had never heard. Experts say that the memory of Alzheimer's sufferers can be prolonged by talking to them about subjects near and dear to their hearts. For Wally, these were scriptures and old country music.

On one occasion, the four of us took a trip about eighty miles north to Liberty, Mississippi. Upon arrival at his sister-in-law's house, we all exchanged pleasantries, and the ladies drifted off to themselves. Wally gave me that look and told them, "We'll be back." Linda and Mary knew what we were up to, just Wally and I doing something together we enjoyed. It gave him a change of pace, something Linda appreciated. For me, watching in curious wonder at this disease slowly taking my friend from me was another Habakkuk moment that God had called me to be a witness of.

We got in the truck without a particular place to go, but I figured that we would take a ride to Brookhaven, about twenty miles east. However, about five miles outside Brookhaven, it started raining, and by the time we got to the edge of town, it was coming down sideways. We both looked at each other, and our eyes locked, silently communicating that we needed to turn around.

When we covered about five miles going back to Liberty, it stopped raining. I resumed the posted fifty-five-mile-per-hour speed, but about halfway back, he shouted, "Turn right! Turn right. This is a shortcut back to Lois's house."

Now we were already in the country, but this shortcut road was even *countrier*. The farther we drove, the skinnier and not as well-maintained the road became. We even got to the point where the road was covered by a canopy of trees.

That was when the reality of my situation struck me. I was taking directions from a man with Alzheimer's but one who I loved like a father. So without him knowing what I was doing, I punched up Google Maps on my phone to see where we were headed. Lucky for me, I had sufficient phone signal to use the app, and sure enough, directly ahead of us over a small rise was the intersection that he knew of and that I had been *greatly* anticipating. I stopped at the stop sign and turned left, and we pulled up in the yard a couple of miles later. It was amazing that my friend remembered this old route.

These types of trips for him and me became less frequent as his condition worsened to the point where he needed professional help. That soon gave way to being placed in a veteran's home an hour's drive away. This was not an easy decision for anyone involved, especially Wally.

The day when he was to be brought to his new home away from home arrived, with lots of routines and processes to learn. On that day, after the customary orientation, with his wife, Linda, having traveled back home, she called me. She told me how the day had gone and how hard it was to leave him there, and then she shared a moment with me that has been described as one of God's tender mercies.

On the front of the property where this veteran's home was located, there still sat a navy jet situated next to the highway for all to see, just like the one that Wally and I visited a few months earlier. Linda, already in an emotional state because of the day's events, with an audible lump in her throat said, "Jim, Wally can see the jet from his room." Now the significance of the earlier visit to the plane in Satsuma, Louisiana, became monumental in my mind.

A few weeks later, Linda, Mary, and I paid Wally a visit. We walked into the facility where the staff, having anticipated our visit, brought him to eat lunch in a dayroom where we could sit together. Again, after a few words of greeting, we took a few pictures, and *poof,* the ladies took off to do some visiting and staff introductions.

Wally checked to make sure that they were out of sight and then motioned for me to move closer, and then he started to whisper, "Jim, you wanna go finishing tomorrow?"

"Sure, I do. I'll pick you up at 5:00 a.m. How about that?"

And just like that, our plans were set.

Wally was grinning from ear to ear as the ladies walked back up. Wally was fit to be tied as he exuberantly exclaimed, "Linda, Jim and I are going fishing in the morning."

Now I quickly turned toward Linda and eyeball to eyeball told her that we were, indeed, going fishing. Though difficult for me to do, I said this harshly to her knowing that if I had not, she would begin to chastise him unnecessarily. I continued my stare and simply whispered, "Later," to her.

I turned back to Wally and told him that I would see him in the morning.

After we said our goodbyes, exchanged hugs, and did the hand sign for *I love you* and of course his iconic "this guy loves you," our visit ended. Linda was now noticeably angry as we rounded the corner and inquired as to why I let him believe that he was going fishing.

"Linda, Wally has always wanted for him and me to go fishing together, but it never happened. Right now, he is excited and thinks he is going to the coast to fish for some speckled trout with his friend. Let him have his moment, and for you, Linda, that smile to remember him by. In an hour, he will have forgotten about it. Linda, remember that smile. I know I will."

We saw my friend one more time before he received his final reward. Part of this story about my friend Wally is among the four or five stories that I submitted to the local paper in Baton Rouge, Louisiana. It was published before Wally died.

Now watch God.

The next morning after its publication, I went to our local pharmacy to pick up a prescription for my wife. As I approached the counter, the pharmacist bellowed, "Hello, Mr. Rioux. I'll have your wife's medicine ready in just a few minutes."

As I turned toward the waiting area, there was an elderly lady seated directly in front of me. She quietly asked, "Are you the James Rioux who wrote that beautiful article in yesterday's paper?"

"Yes, ma'am, I am," I replied.

Then in the sweetest, yet emotional voice, she simply said, "Thank you."

If that heartfelt expression of appreciation, given by a stranger who obviously was dealing with the pain of watching a loved one go through Alzheimer's, is the only reward that I will ever receive, it is enough. In fact, that lady's kind words have been one of the greatest sources of encouragement for me to continue writing and posting on social media. I was very fortunate to see her and hear her words of gratitude. I have to think that many more have seen my stories without personally expressing their gratitude to me.

The use of my God-given gift of telling a story in written words is all that God asked me to do. It is my knowledge that as God inspired and prepared me to write that story weeks earlier, He was also creating the opportunity, with many moving parts, for that sweet lady and me to come face-to-face. Our spiritual gifts are not ours to keep; we are to give them away—willingly.

And he said unto them, Go ye into all the world, and preach the gospel to every creature.

—Mark 16:15 KJV

FATHER, ARE YOU THERE?

If there had ever been someone in my life who encouraged me to do my part in spreading the gospel, it was Wally. With that, I decided to include here in Wally's story another story of an exceptionally long-distance influence on someone's life and mine through my writing.

It has always been my way of "preaching" that isn't really preaching at all. I write posts on Facebook intended for the readers to simply look over my shoulder and watch what I do and for them to observe how I live my life. I have never pointed a finger and told someone what they should do but just simply say, "This is my experience."

I'm not perfect and not an expert on any subject matter, but with eight billion on the planet, 25 percent of them are active daily users of Facebook. Among those two billion people theoretically looking over my shoulder, at least a few can relate to me—how I do and what I do—and be emboldened to do things similarly.

In fact, the person I will mention here just interacted with me about a post I put up this morning. I take that as a confirmation that including it here has God's approval.

It has long been my experience that when we share our life with others on social media, we may never know

1. who is watching,

2. why they are watching, or
3. for how long.

I have believed for a long time, I have been instructed by the Holy Ghost to write, post, and then repeat daily. My calling is to write, and though I post it on a global network, God is truly in charge of the distribution. He prepares me to write while He prepares others to see it, just like the sweet, elderly lady at the pharmacy who saw my newspaper article.

One morning in February 2017 at four-thirty, I received a direct message from Jemael on Facebook Messenger.

Father, are you there? it read.

I quickly looked up this person whose name I did not recognize but who was on my friend list. In fact, we had been friends for a year almost to that day. He was from the country Côte d'Ivoire in West Africa. It was 10:30 a.m. in his time zone. This was the first time that he has messaged me.

I answered, not knowing why he was referring to me as *father*, *Yes, Jemael, I am here.*

Father, I have a problem, he continued.

Yes, Jemael. How can I help?

Father, I do not like the church that I belong to. I need your advice.

At that point, I resisted the urge to tell him about my church. I knew absolutely nothing of his situation, which church he attended, nothing. Later, I would learn that he was nineteen years old, both his parents were deceased, he was raising his younger siblings with the help of an uncle, and he was impoverished without work.

And then I was prompted to simply ask him to read one verse of scripture. *Jemael, do you read the Bible?"*

Yes, sir. I do, he replied.

Do you think that you can find James 1:5?

Yes, sir.

Can you read and pray about it and then message me again tomorrow at this same time?

Yes, Father.

James 1:5 is one of the simplest biblical teachings for one who seeks divine direction or any direction at all. "If any of you lack wisdom, let them ask of God."

Jemael had been watching my posts for a year. He, I suppose, had been searching for someone he could trust, someone who was consistent with their content. He was searching for someone who was not sending mixed signals with spiritual posts one day and then off-color or even a vulgar post the next day. He probably wanted more than a website's autoresponder. He still calls me *father*, and I still do not know why. I have not asked, and I call him *son*.

The next morning at exactly four-thirty, I received a message: *Father, are you there?*

I replied, *Yes, Jemael. I am here. Did you read James 1:5?'*

His short, simple reply was, *Yes, I did.*

I asked him, *Well?*

Thank you.

That was 2017. With over five thousand miles between us, we still interact regularly on Facebook.

Subsequently, I have also learned that his desire was to preach and teach the Bible. I asked why he could not do that, and he told me that he didn't have a church and didn't know how to build a following. When I asked him how he found me, he said, "Through Facebook." I continued asking what would stop him from just getting online and talking about his relationship with God to his friends and that he could start a Facebook group and conduct Facebook live broadcasts. I suggested that he simply do what he and I were doing. I told him that anytime he had doubts or questions, just go back to James 1:5.

I soon saw him building a group, preaching, and teaching and tagging me on his posts. Life has not been easy for Jemael for many reasons, one of which is that his country is predominately Muslim in the north and Christian in the south, with many areas of western Africa experiencing bloodshed and entire Christian villages being burned by radical Muslims, resulting in the deaths of many Christians.

Jemael perseveres, facing many adversities that we do not experience here in America. I hope to meet this young man one day. He has been another in a long line of people who inspire and encourage me to continue to write.

"We may never know who is watching, for how long or why."

Much love,
—Paw Paw

For I know the plans I have for you, declares the Lord, plans to prosper you and not harm you, plans to give you a hope and a future.

—Jeremiah 29:11KJV

THIRD TABLE

That Old House

All that I can say is thanks. Many instructive lessons were encapsulated as acts of love, patience, and discipline in that old house. Adversity was sometimes dealt with through the quiet solitude that served as the de-escalation of a bad situation, sometimes not.

In its first life with the Rioux name on courthouse records, it housed one set of parents, seven boys, and two girls. Of the nine children, the last two were twins, with my father always telling friends that he and Momma stopped growing the family when they started coming two at a time. Also in the head count were a string of dogs and many cats.

Getting along involved going along, as in eating what Momma put on the table, wearing what was provided, and never having enough seating on Saturday night at the movies on NBC when there were only three TV channels. We had one couch and two extra chairs other than Mom's and Dad's, the only reserved seating in the living room.

The younger ones watched from the floor, no carpet, but that was what we did unless the company visited, which put a couple more kids on the floor. If we complained, Mom responded with her now-iconic reply, "You'll live."

My dad's favorite show was *The Silent Service*. It was about navy submarines. When the show came on, one of us would scream, "Daddy, ah-ooga, ah-ooga. Dive! Dive! is coming on." Momma's favorite was any variety show with Pete Fountain playing jazz on his clarinet or Roy Clark playing his guitar.

My favorite was *Mister Ed*, the talking horse. It was on TV on Sundays, and I came in once and changed the TV channel so I could watch it. I, of course, was screamed at for switching off the predecessor to the Super Bowl. These were the days of Red Skelton and Ed Sullivan. *The Jackie Gleason Show*, as I remember, was too risqué for our family.

With little ones straddling the limited floor space, the only scary moments came when 910 WLCS, the local top-forty radio station had a "Name It and Claim It" contest with the ninth caller winning a 45 RPM record (google that one, kids). If Paul, son number 2, child number 3, was in his bedroom at the end of the hall when the contest was announced, he would come running at full speed, stepping over and around terrified young ones like a football player running the tires at practice.

I do not remember any of us getting stepped on or him ever winning the coveted record, only complaining that with an ancient rotary phone (google that one too), he would never be able to beat those rich kids with the new touch-tone phones. Again, of course, Mom would say, "You'll live."

Back in the day, before they put a stop sign at the intersection of Ray Weiland and Cypress in the Bakersfield subdivision in my Louisiana hometown, the same brother would sometimes come in after curfew. With his less-than-quiet, nineteen-whatever German-made Vauxhall stick transmission, he would turn left off Main Street, cross the railroad tracks, accelerate just enough to get to the little hill in the curve past the laundromat, kill the engine in neutral, and coast through the intersection and then quietly into the driveway to not to be detected coming home late by Papa Bear. Sometimes it worked, and sometimes it did not, but the challenge was always worth the effort.

After we first got married, my wife asked if I had taken a shower on a certain occasion. I told her that I had, with her exclaiming, "Jim, there is no way. You were only in there for five minutes." I would then reply that it was actually less than five minutes with a follow-up explanation. I would then tell the story of the waterlines that broke in the foundation of the old house where I grew up, which required my dad and me to reroute around the house to the utility room. When he reconnected the line to the water heater, he put a hand valve on it. With nine people living in this old house at the time, hot water had to be rationed, which meant that when we were in the shower for four minutes, he would knock on the shared wall between the kitchen and the one bathroom. At five minutes, the hot water was turned off. A sudden cold shower, especially in the winter, was one of those instructive lessons mentioned earlier.

I learned to never underestimate the athletic abilities of a mother of nine children. I worked at a local grocery store at age fourteen. My boss would allow me to bring home eggs that were collected from cartons with broken ones. They were transferred into empty cartons that the egg company provided. My boss charged me ten cents a dozen, as I recall.

One night, I devised a plan to trick my mother when I brought home empty cartons. The setup was that I would call ahead of time so that she would know I was bringing home some eggs. I got home, balanced the empty cartons in my arms, and then nudged the back door open, screaming for her to help me because they were falling from my grasp.

She was sitting at the sewing machine across the kitchen and told me to just put them on the kitchen table. After pleading with her again for some help, she stopped what she was doing and started to get up. At this point, I acted like I was falling as I tossed the empty cartons her way, with each of them flying in four different directions. It was now her turn to holler, so I took off down the hall to the back bedroom.

This old house had eight-foot ceilings, and somehow, with one fell swoop, she was able to reach down, grab a shoe, and hurl it like a major league baseball pitcher the entire length of the house and strike me in the butt before I could make my turn into the bedroom. Never ever underestimate your mother.

My oldest sibling, Valerie, was a nursing student and initially lived on campus without a car. This would require the Sunday night ritual of bringing her to school, after the *Red Skelton Comedy Hour*, of course, you know, back when families watched the same channel—together—IN THE SAME ROOM.

The route to Val's school would take us south on Scenic Highway before I-110 was built, not long after the dinosaurs disappeared. We would pass Hopper's Drive-In and turn right on Chippewa, which prompted a varying number of the children present to scream, "Dad, honk the horn!," and he knew that meant under the railroad underpass. This simple pleasure of ours brought such joy because the horn would make a loud echo. It's not as exciting when I do it these days. YES, I STILL DO IT.

Valerie eventually got an apartment, with two or three roommates, and her own car, and it was not just any car; it was a blue 1966 1/2 or 1967 navy blue Ford Mustang. There was much-shared love for that car as she would occasionally take one of us on trips to the grocery store. It was such a cool car.

However, she traded it a few years later for a Ford LTD. We still love our sister so much; she helped raise the younger ones before her nursing career bloomed. But an LTD? Really? Hindsight is a son of a bugger, and it's easy to look back now and question that decision, but an LTD for a classic Mustang?

All nine of us children attended the local schools in that old house in Baker, a northern suburb of Baton Rouge. The three older siblings attended elementary school in Massachusetts, the state in which my father was born and raised. My mother grew up in Baton Rouge but graduated from the same high school in Baker from which all her children graduated. During my mom's years as a Baker Buffalo, there were only eleven grades when some of the teachers rode a train from Baton Rouge into our small town.

The rite of passage for most of the boys was to get a job at fourteen or fifteen years of age at a local grocery store for some walking-around money and to pay our part of the one family car insurance premium; you drive, you pay. We would also bring home day-old bread at a low, low price or other food items that would help stretch the family budget.

BOB AND MARY

My mother and father met at a navy base south of New Orleans around the time of the Normandy invasion during World War II. He was a member of the Merchant Marines and was from Massachusetts. My mother had traveled with a couple of friends from Baton Rouge to New Orleans for some shopping. The trip for some of the single ladies at the time involved going to lunch at the naval base commissary, of course, because of the excellent food (wink wink) and an equally excellent chance of meeting one of the young, single, dapper-looking military types.

As these three young ladies were thus engaged in their meal, one of them, Ms. Juanita, called one young man over to the table and asked if he might join them. He obliged and sat next to Ms. Juanita, to which she exclaimed, "Not next to me. Sit by this pretty one." She then pointed to my future mom. My mother and future dad hit it off wonderfully and were soon married.

At some point, after they married, after the war, and before they moved to Massachusetts, a circumstance was explained to me by my father. It involved him having a job in Baton Rouge, driving a truck. On one trip, he remembered driving through Baker on Groom Road, which runs adjacent to the subdivision in which that old house is now located. He remembered noticing the property as being barren of any homes at that time, property that would within a few years contain that old house and many others.

On that same road, adjacent to our subdivision, is a bridge that spans a drainage canal. Upon returning to Louisiana from Massachusetts with the young family in tow, my father had left work at a chemical plant in Baton Rouge within hours of the landfall of a major 1960s hurricane. He and another worker listened to traffic reports of known routes that were not yet closed because of high water and determined that they would leave together and come to Baker the "back way" via Scenic Highway and then down that same Groom Road with the little wooden bridge. My dad made it safely home but did not hear from his coworker who had not been far behind him until their next time at work.

When they saw each other again, he asked my dad, "Bob, how did you make it home?"

"I went down Groom Road, crossed the bridge, and turned into the subdivision as we had discussed," he replied.

"Bob, by the time I got to the bridge, it had washed out."

It was just another example of how God is in control.

Speaking of hurricanes, while my parents' concern was for our safety during a storm, we as kids never realized the many other things that they were worried about until we got older, like a tree falling on the house or some other major damage. But my father, after we lost electricity, would always seem to find the time to entertain the children as a distraction from the howling winds by making hand-shadow figures on the wall from the light of the hurricane lamp. Maybe it was a distraction for him too!

One of the most clear and profound lessons I was taught was never spoken; it was learned through observation; it was demonstrated. My father taught me how to treat a wife.

I never heard them argue in front of us, and man-and-wife discussions were done in private. I never heard him speak ugly words to her or threaten her in any way. I never saw him handle her in a vulgar manner in front of us. And he was always sure to allow us to witness him giving her affectionate but tame kisses and hugs.

There are far too many stories to tell that involve the first Rioux era in that old house. Five out of the nine children were born at some point after moving to that old house in 1958. My siblings and I presented twenty-three grandchildren to my parents in that old house over the years; there was lots of love sprinkled with adversity, both of which were nourishment for each of us to carry to the next generation.

My mother overheard a couple of us looking through her high school annual. Upon finding her picture in a tenth-grade class photo, one of us said, "That's Momma back when she was pretty." She would laugh every time she heard that story.

Then in 1987, my father died on the property. My mother had gone to the grocery store. My sister called to find out what he wanted for Father's Day on the coming Sunday. He said he wanted a Mercedes-Benz; his humor was evident right up to the end. They had spoken at 2:00 p.m., as she clearly remembers. At 2:10 p.m., Momma returned from the grocery store and found him outside. He had died very quickly of a heart attack and had attempted to get to a neighbor's house. I have to think that he died laughing, the way he would have wanted to.

My mother went to a nursing home, but before she died, she was moved to a brother's home, whose wife was a nurse who could assist the home health nurses who attended to my mother. This gave all the children and grandchildren the chance to experience what can be a very beautiful journey to witness as one slips from this earthly home to an eternal mansion that awaits them. My mother deserved one of those mansions.

Each of us had opportunities to speak to her, unlike my father's quick and unexpected death. Some read poetry or notes to her from those who could not travel to be by her side. Some sang childhood songs that she sang to us as infants.

When my parents first met at that naval base, he was a Merchant Marine handsomely attired in his uniform, standing along a counter next to the restaurant. After they were married, this couple loved to dance, among other things, which continued for many years.

Many experts suggest that when speaking to someone in my mother's advanced stage, it is beneficial to permit them to "go." In all honesty, to me, it sounded like kicking an old lady down the steps, but that's just me. So on the third night at my brother's home before her death, I began to ask her if she was ready to dance with the "sailor at the counter." On this night, she gave an explicit *no*. The next night, it was the same but a little milder. The next night, a couple hours prior to her passing, I asked her once again, "Mom, are you ready to dance with that sailor at the counter?"

On this night, she nodded in approval. She knew, as so many do. Then she joined her waiting sailor as he welcomed her home across the veil.

The second Rioux era began with my wife, Mary, after I inherited that old house. I remarried and chose a lady whom a neighbor would refer to as the second Mary, my mother being the first Mary in that old house. The second Mary and I spent twenty years there, created many happy moments, endured a few adversarial ones, added to the headcount of dogs and cats that lived there, and threw in some parrots for good measure. She also continued the tradition of sewing in that old house. She loved putting up strawberry preserves and making everything from scratch.

My children had a hard time getting used to her North Carolina terminology for things. Mary once asked my daughter Annie to go into the kitchen and bring her "pocketbook" into the living room. I let it go for a few minutes as Annie searched high and low for Mary's pocketbook. After she became frustrated, she told Mary that she couldn't find her pocketbook, at which point I told her to just bring Mary's purse. Annie replied, "Oh, her purse is right here."

These stories, among many others, stand out the strongest to me from that old house.

A neighbor seemed to have been told that the houses on the block were built somewhere near 1950. This one had never been updated; the same round screw-in fuses in the electric box, two-prong electric outlets, windows, walls, and floors all needed replacing.

I sold that old house, not for what my family would think, to an investor who called unsolicited, a man sent by God for sure, sent to bug me until we agreed on a price—a price far below my expectations.

He upgraded the electrical; put in its first central air; redid those walls, floors, and windows; put on a new roof; trimmed the many tree branches away; tore down the carport that did not need much help to be accomplished; rebuilt the added-on utility room that I helped my dad with (with a little help, I might add); and redid the bathroom—among other things, I am sure. He rented it out for retirement income. Good for him.

After having bought a mobile home "across the riva," as my grandkids would say, my daughters and I spoke of new beginnings, fresh starts, and a new life, as it were. One daughter, as stated earlier, having read me the riot act, encouraged me forcefully to begin writing this book. I will write full-time after retiring on social security in a few months in that new place, one I now call "La Maison de Rougon."

But that old house, filled with many worn-out but still-vivid stories, caused me at the closing, very unexpectedly and unrehearsed, to get a little emotional with the investor, reflecting on the new beginning that the old house would experience.

You see, this neighborhood that I grew up in was filled during the '50s and '60s with young families just starting out, doing their best to make it from paycheck to paycheck. Some of the kids I grew up with in the neighborhood still live there, having inherited their "old house"—their childhood home.

However, with the sale of that old house and the subsequent restoration, there is a young family right now, not known to themselves but only to God, that will experience their new beginning, their fresh start, and their new life precipitated by a real estate agent that has helped other young couples realize their dream of living in a real home, not an apartment or Section 8 housing.

They might be looking at a house at a scary monthly cost, but the dream is the same with every aspiring young couple—a home with a yard for the kids, many dogs and cats, dads throwing the football with the boys, little girls having a tea party, friends camping out in the backyard, girls having sleepovers, crayon writing on the same walls that a sister of mine covered up with wallpaper that erased years of our childhood hieroglyphics, dads with their workshop, and moms with a sewing or crafts room.

The ethnic background of this family may be different from mine, but the challenge is the same as it was in the '50s and '60s: struggling paycheck to paycheck, or rather, direct deposit to direct deposit, with used cars with aging tires, lots of beans and rice, and hand-me-down clothes. This investor will create a new home where all these things will be possible.

I shared this little vision of mine with the investor across that big table in front of a slightly impatient closing agent. I paused, looked the man in the eyes one more time, and asked him to do his best to make a young family's dream come true. And maybe—just maybe—on a long shot, at least one of the renters' names will be Mary, Mary number 3.

That old house where dreams were ignited and where children learned many life skills and adversity de-escalation skills—that old house is not approaching an end but a beginning.

Much love,
—Paw Paw

I'm writing my story so that others might see fragments of themselves.

—Lena Waithe, screenwriter

LAST TABLE

My Angel

I found myself back then in my big truck in her part of the country on a regular basis. I always seemed to be en route from a chemical plant or paper mill in South Louisiana to the northeastern corridor of the United States on any given week. One of my favorite stops was a truck stop in Fort Chiswell, Virginia, because of the reliable food; you learned to take it when you could get it.

Before I started losing brain cells after my recent sixty-fifth birthday, I could tell you at least the month of the year that I first laid eyes on her—Mary by name.

It was her blue, soul-piercing eyes that first caught my attention. I must have appeared ragged to her with my disorganized beard and the equally confusing aroma of my Michael Jordan knockoff cologne from a dollar store that attempted to mask the effects of three days without a shower that hovered around me. Back in those days, a truck driver would have to consider using three hours of what was then a required eight-hour rest break waiting for a shower to become available or forgoing the shower for a full night's rest. Today, we have a ten-hour break with many more truck stops dotting the highways. With those changes, truck drivers look and smell better today, and they get more rest. Thank goodness.

I was divorced and discovered very quickly how ineffective a flirt I was. Even though I quickly got up to speed after the divorce was final, I was even worse at the follow-up line to a seemingly positive response.

A quick example of this was when a lady, also in Virginia, told me that she loved the smell of my dollar store cologne. Before I knew what I was about to say, I blurted out, "Sure, but would you take me home and make me biscuits?"

She firmly responded, "Yes."

With that, I responded with absolutely nothing. I did not have a response to a positive answer of any kind. There was nothing left to do but walk away, licking my emotional wounds. Sales professionals say that the gold is in the follow-up. There was no gold for me on that day.

But there I was at the truck stop in Fort Chiswell, looking into these beautiful blue eyes, and on this occasion, our first meeting, our conversation started much like the other one when Mary also told me that I smelled good, which meant that she, too, had poor taste in cologne.

I told her that I sure hoped that her sweetie appreciated her blue eyes. She then painted a very bleak picture of her situation and made a condescending remark about her appearance, but she thanked me for my kind words. She was a woman who would escape a second look from many guys; most were looking for a Barbie-type. Maybe both of us were too old for that. She was looking for an emotionally supportive partner, and I was searching for a grandmotherly type, the type that could make me and my grandchildren biscuits; well, she could, and she made them from scratch, which I would eventually learn—no cans popping on the edge of the counter for her.

She was a convenience store clerk at this truck stop. We finished our conversation and then asked for a key and towel for a shower, and I was gone. I went back looking for her the next time I found myself on I-81 over the next few months. I seemed to have just missed her on several occasions, but I persevered, and about five months later, I found her on duty at midnight. This was only after saying hello to her and having to walk by her several times before she recognized me. I guess if you have seen one truck driver, you have seen them all.

We proceeded to talk off and on for four hours, taking a break when the boss was in the area. She remembered later that we talked every day on the phone thereafter until she moved for a brief period to live with her mom.

We eventually married in my native Louisiana. Ours was not a perfect marriage, to say the least, with many medical issues that caused a never-ending physical strain on her eventually debilitating condition and, of course, a financial strain with her many hospitalizations, allergies, history of pneumonia, and taking twenty-two medications per day that led to her life-ending kidney failure.

She was a very spiritual person and loved God and our church, but her emotional issues presented our marriage with many significant challenges. I was not prepared to deal with this level of constant issues caused by depression. I loved her immensely and did everything I could to comfort her and help her through her tough days. But even the immense love, I soon found, was not enough to strengthen her.

I very carefully but honestly state here that she did not do all that she was capable of, even with God's loving care and kindness, to take care of her health. She always resorted to another doctor with a better pill or another improved therapy.

An incredibly wise nutritionist told me about five years before Mary died that the many prescriptions that she was taking would be a contributing factor to her eventual demise because of the toxic medications' harm to the kidneys. In conjunction with her inattention to her diabetes, when the time came later for her to be considered for dialysis, the doctors said that her system was just too weak and compromised.

There were people whom we considered friends who, having seen firsthand the behavior caused by her depression, had seriously suggested that I should consider divorcing her. As I was writing this chapter, I saw a quote by a long-married couple that said that they came from a generation that fixed things when they seemed irreparable, including marriage. I always seem to remember a part of the marriage vows that say, "In good times and bad." Geez, call me old-fashioned.

Before I go any further, full disclosure: I am not perfect, surprise, surprise. I have my aggravating idiosyncrasies. I am a truck driver, gone for days and weeks at a time. It is not the kind of occupation well suited to be of support for a diabetic with depression. But I persevered as well, as expected.

Somewhere about halfway through our twenty-two-year marriage, I became curious about the finer points of nutrition, organic supplementation, healthy eating, and the toxicities that we unknowingly put into our bodies every day. I did this in association with a company that I marketed for as a side gig. This is how I helped myself lose one hundred pounds, and this nutrition company is where I met and was taught by a world-class nutritionist.

In a brief exchange with my wife, not long after being told this by the nutritionist, Mary looked me directly in the eyes and said, "Jim, you may know a lot about nutrition, but don't you dare tell me how to live my life."

That bit of rebuke was only a foreshadowing of the things that I found around our home after she passed in areas where I was forbidden to go looking—things like her secret stashes of Hershey's Kisses, unused and unopened glucose test strips, and monitors.

In the "sewing room" closet, I found cloth and sewing patterns never used, amounting to hundreds of dollars. I also found a similar worth of school and office supplies to feed her office supply fetish, over twenty pairs of the same pair of sewing scissors. I say twenty only because that is where I stopped counting.

I was especially told to stay out of the back or junk room. She did not want me cleaning and straightening in there without her help, even when it became impossible for her to do so because of her later health condition. When she moved her stuff into the house, she brought her granny's old White rotary sewing machine and a portable tabletop model.

After her passing, I started going through the house, sorting, throwing away, and starting a corner with the things I was to keep. In the corner of the junk room, under a pile designed as a bit of subterfuge, I found two more sewing machines I knew nothing of.

In looking back on the time spent in the house by herself, mostly alone because of her husband's absence, I have, out of necessity, rationalized the candy, office supplies, cloth inventory, and sewing machines as a form of therapeutic creature comforts for someone with depression that I had greatly underestimated. Looking back on it now, dwelling on these things would have driven me crazy. These things brought her joy even as her health began to spiral out of control. Having discussed these consequences many times together, I have since realized this was the path she had chosen. I have also thought that these things have been set aside as a form of visual hope. In conjunction with her lack of attention to her health, I have since been made to understand that for Mary, as the thought of any semblance of recovery became overwhelming, all these things collectively were a part of what giving up looked like.

I must admit that the weeping and mourning after her death soon morphed into anger. I did begin to dwell on the years with her that had been stolen from me. Death is inevitable for all of us, but this is not how I expected to spend our final years together. I wanted more time with a woman I absolutely adored.

Today, I cannot look at someone walking a dog without thinking that Mary would think it was cute. I cannot see an airplane taking off from the many airports I pass without remembering that she would be screaming in excitement, suffice it to say that she loved airplanes, especially if she was a passenger. I cannot look at the St. Louis Arch which I pass frequently without remembering that we kissed underneath that "Gateway to the West." I see these things and, even today, still find myself reaching for the phone to call her.

I loved her even when those around me could not understand. I loved her even as I saw her destroying herself with a lack of concern for her own well-being. I loved her even as I began to question how I could stay devoted to a person who obviously lacked devotion to her own longevity.

"For better or worse, till death do us part." Some would say that I persevered to a fault. I somehow found the physical and emotional strength to push through another day, through another weekend that found me walking in the door and not sitting down until the day was done, collapsing on the side of the bed in exhaustion, having to do everything I could to make things easier for her when I was gone. Maybe that was the wrong thing to do—maybe, maybe, maybe.

It came to a point, especially after her rebuke instructing me not to tell her how to live her life, that our marriage began to feel like an assignment from God for me to do all within my power to comfort her as physically and emotionally as possible. At some point, she decided that the road to sufficiently improving her habits was too daunting a task. In the end, I felt that I had met the obligation of my assignment to help her prolong her own life, even as I sat in her final hospice room with my daughter, waiting for the coroner's office to come and collect her now lifeless body, beautiful blue eyes, and all.

I speak here of these unpleasant things that were certainly interspersed with many of the happiest times of our life together so that I may demonstrate the proper context surrounding some of the events near the end of her life. These events contained evidence of God's exquisite love and timing for His imperfect children. These occurrences of these events and the placement of certain people within her sphere could only have been accomplished by a loving God in heaven.

These things were for her and her alone during her walk toward the other side of the veil. My part in all of this at the end was simply to be part of her support system and be a Habakkuk-like witness to all these events, good and bad, as God's chosen scribe for her, including some that occurred after she had earned her eternal reward.

I would like it to be clearly understood that, as I understand God's love for us, He will always love the sinner but not the sin. In my imperfect daily walk with the Savior, it has been my understanding that we are required to take care of our bodies, our temple, to the best of our abilities. I do not consider her or anyone else a sinner for not eating properly. While it was my personal witness that this woman whom I adored did not demonstrate her best efforts in the matter of her own health, I must state unequivocally that, indeed, I am not her judge.

Based on the account that I will mention later in this chapter, I knew that Mary was at peace with God, leading up to the process of crossing over to the other side.

Through it all, I still loved her dearly, and God's love for her never ceases, as evidenced by the following stories.

Mary Elisabeth Rioux

A FAMILY
RESEARCH TRIP

Mary loved doing family history work, which was done in association with the performance of church ordinances. She had been planning for some time to take one of many trips home to North Carolina to visit with relatives and have them fill out a family history questionnaire. She especially wanted to see her favorite, Uncle Charles, her mother's brother.

I came home one Tuesday afternoon about eleven or twelve years ago. She had her plane ticket in hand when she took a call from her sister and walked into the back of the house. She had been on the phone for a while, at least so I thought, so I went back to the bedroom to check on her.

There I found her on the edge of the bed, weeping.

"What is wrong?" I asked.

Through her tears, she blurted out, "Uncle Charles died."

After a few minutes of attempting to console her, the crying got worse. I tried to understand her worsening sobs when she reminded me that she was leaving Thursday to go back home, especially to visit him about family history.

"Mary?" I asked, "You're still going, aren't you?"

"Why?" she replied loudly. "Uncle Charles is dead. He's gone. He is the one person I wanted to go see."

I waited for a few minutes. Her weeping subsided somewhat, and I hugged her a little tighter and delicately asked, "Mary, when does the viewing at the funeral home begin?"

A suggestion of aggravation was pointed in my direction as she asked, "Why do you ask me that?"

I continued, "Mary, who is going to be at the funeral home paying respects?"

Still, just a little perturbed at me, she responded, "Family!" at which point, the countenance on her face changed for the better. A slight smile broke across her face.

"Mary, don't you think that you should make some extra copies of your questionnaire?"

She collected her composure and then began to pack her suitcase, and two days later, she flew to North Carolina for the wake and funeral.

AN OLDER GENTLEMAN

She attended the wake on Friday at the appointed time, was able to visit with many relatives she had not seen in many years, and received a lot of family history information.

As the attendees started to leave, with the crowd thinning out, she and her sister noticed a much older man standing across the room by himself. Mary asked her sister if that man did not look like a member of the Lee family, their mother's family name. Her sister told her no and that all the members of that generation were dead and gone.

Still curious, they walked over to him and inquired about his name. "Lee," he responded. Indeed, here was a member of a generation thought to be long deceased. Mary explained her purpose for this trip in addition to the wake of her uncle Charles, that being family history research, and asked him if he would fill out her questionnaire.

Now watch God! He said that he could do something even better.

"Would you two come by the house tomorrow? I have something to show you, something that you might be interested in seeing," the older gentleman said.

Now these two sisters had heard their mother for years tell them about some well-known ancestors in the family line but were not so sure of the story's validity.

They arrived at this relative's home the Sunday after the funeral and were asked to be seated at the kitchen table while he went into the back of the house to retrieve "some things." Upon his return, he placed a briefcase on the table in front of them and started carefully laying out some old documents and papers in front of them.

All these years, their mother had told them the story of being related to General Robert E. Lee of Civil War notoriety, and now sitting in front of them was the proof. But this relative kept pulling more items out of this family's historical vault disguised as a simple attaché case.

What was revealed to Mary and her sister was the unknown connection between their mother, the general, and the Declaration of Independence. Two ancestors of Robert E. Lee were Richard Henry Lee, an American statesman and one of the Founding Fathers of the United States, as well as being best known (according to Wikipedia) for the June 1776 Lee Resolution, the motion in the Continental Congress calling for the colonies' independence from Great Britain, which led to the Declaration of Independence, which he also signed.

The documentation identified his brother, Francis Lightfoot Lee, as also a signer of this American historical document. Furthermore, these two ladies were shown a copy of a handwritten account of Francis Lightfoot Lee having been the one who originally put quill to paper as the words were dictated to him by John Adams, Benjamin Franklin, Thomas Jefferson, Roger Sherman, and Robert Livingston. At some point, Thomas Jefferson tapped Francis Lightfoot Lee on the shoulder and suggested that he thought that he could write a little better than Lightfoot.

As this older gentleman continued showing them this rich deposit of family history, they were in awe and shock. And to think that it may never have been made known to the family if Mary had continued to cry on the bed five days earlier and not made the trip or if Mary and her sister had just agreed that the older man across the funeral parlor was not a long-forgotten member of the Lee ancestry and left.

Look at God!

ANOTHER TRIP TO NORTH CAROLINA

I have never had an exceptionally good memory when it comes to dates, but suffice it to say that about seven years prior to Mary's passing, she had flown to see her daughter in North Carolina. She loved to fly and hated to have to take the airline tags off her suitcases; they were her souvenirs.

This trip was not unusual in that it also included a trip to the hospital for swelling in her right foot. On at least one other occasion, she spent a few days in the hospital there because of her recurring bouts with pneumonia. At first, the prognosis on this doctor's trip was a bug bite, but the medication that had been called for did not seem to alleviate the swelling. With diabetes, one must always be aware of the condition of their feet, and this episode was not any different.

As a last-minute afterthought on the second visit, the doctor suggested taking an X-ray, during which he found a hairline fracture in her foot. Accompanying her diabetes was neuropathy, a loss of feeling in her feet, so she had no recollection of pain associated with an injury-causing misstep during her visit.

The doctor suggested that she not fly back home but that I was to drive the sixteen hours from Louisiana to pick her up. This round trip was accomplished in a matter of three days, after which, a five-year doctor-patient relationship with her orthopedic surgeon commenced. Again, the healing process during her four upcoming foot surgeries was exacerbated by diabetes, which meant an extended healing process. During these surgeries, many screws, plates, and wires were attached to her foot.

It was my less-than-scientific opinion that her continued health issues were made worse by a weak immune system and not helped a bit by her poor eating habits. It also seemed to me that these complicated foot issues began her downward health spiral. The fact that could not be ignored was that she was a tough lady through all these surgical episodes.

After each surgery, her daily routine involved examining her foot for any signs of infection. Somewhere during this process, closer to the last foot surgery by the orthopedic, she lost her professional affection for her favorite doctor.

Mary did not follow post-surgery protocols when it came to keeping weight off the foot as much as possible, even with the walkers and leg carts that she was given to use. Her continuing nutritional shortcomings all came to a head in a conversation with the three of us during a visit.

Mary's surgeon was also an inventor of some orthopedic footwear and a marathon runner who knew well the prerace preparation required as well as the postrace recovery period necessary. During this visit, I asked her doctor, as an analogy, to explain her processes before and after a race and compared them to Mary's condition. I asked the doctor if it involved putting herself through some uncomfortable or even painful exercises, and she responded in the affirmative. Mary took offense to this line of bedside manner and clearly understood the connection the doctor and I were making to her self-care. Mary never spoke as glowingly about her once-favorite doctor again.

Things got even worse for Mary after the last reconstructive surgery. I noticed some spots on her toes that just did not look right and, in fact, were found to be serious infections that led to her toes on that foot being removed. Given her mobility being reduced in conjunction with her previous surgeries, her continued bouts of pneumonia, and the later to-be-revealed kidney issues, going out about town to take care of shopping chores herself became a thing of the past. She began a season of a more sedentary life.

From that point forward, I did all the prescription pickups and grocery shopping since I was home every two to three days at that time. In addition to her physical issues, I noticed some memory issues that I supposed were related to her many pain medications and the kidneys' inability to filter toxicities as well.

As her condition began to deteriorate, almost imperceptibly, one thing led to another, as the next story explains.

JIM, GO BACK IN THE HOUSE

As her sedentary lifestyle accelerated, her metabolism certainly slowed down. She had always been proud of the way she would keep herself busy while sewing, cooking, putting up fruit preserves, and doing various other activities that kept her active, especially her Facebook lives for her Paparazzi jewelry shows. The slowly manifesting memory issues were visited by periods of confusion, which she had a talent for disguising as simple everyday forgetfulness. She would tell me, "You do the same thing, Jim."

The other condition that arose in her daily routine was longer periods of sleep. When we were first married, she would get into these temporary periods of sluggishness to the point where she would start slurring her words. My son called one night and told me that I needed to come home because Mary was in bad shape. When I got home, her pillbox was in disarray, which meant that she was not taking her medications properly.

At that point, I had to get on the computer to identify each of these fifteen pills and put them in their proper bottles and the pill tray correctly. This began my habit of looking over her medications periodically, calling in refills, and setting up her pill tray before leaving for a few days. She was very independent and did not for a minute appreciate anyone else, including her husband "treating her like a baby."

This incident, however, was not concluded. The next morning, I called the doctor and had him look at her medication chart and see if he could find a reason for her increased sleeping patterns and confusion. Shockingly, his nurse called back within five minutes and then admitted that of the fifteen medications on her chart at the time, seven of them were sedatives. Mary needed to have her prescriptions rewritten to eliminate so many of the sedatives and replace them with something more compatible with one another.

Thus began the process of not only looking over Mary's shoulder but questioning the doctor also. Though her confusion and sluggishness seemed to improve, the extended sleep patterns did not. It then became commonplace for her to not fall asleep until 1:00 a.m. or later in the morning and then to not wake up until as late as noon. This meant that she was sleeping right through the time to eat breakfast, monitor her glucose levels, and take her morning medications. It is quite easy to see how things gradually began to spiral out of control for her over the next few months.

I now fast forward past a few more episodes of her lack of concern for proper eating and taking her medications on time, or even taking them at all. But she never missed her pain medications. She watched them like a hawk. Add that to her lack of diligent concern for checking her blood sugar levels, including taking her insulin at the proper times or in the proper dosage, and the perfect storm was forming inside the body of this blue-eyed angel that I dearly loved.

I am an early riser. I have a tough time sleeping past 5:00 a.m., so it was very commonplace for me to do the housework and cooking as she slept. As she progressively slept longer as her health declined, she began the habit of sleeping the entire night in the living room recliner. This was a blessing in disguise in that I later learned from neighbors the number of times that emergency personnel was sent to our home because a friend was not able to reach her on the phone because of a fall. Sleeping in the bedroom at the end of a hall would have created an issue getting her to a stretcher in our small home.

This period of sleeping in the living room continued for months until an incident not long before her period of rehab occurred. I had done all my chores and needed to go to the grocery store. It was almost 11:00 a.m. when I walked out the door. I tried to wake her up without success. On many occasions, when I awakened her, I would be rebuked instantly. So on this occasion, her deep sleep did not seem unusual. I jumped into the pickup and started backing out of the driveway. As I came to a stop to check for traffic, I had a prompting that almost seemed audible from somewhere behind me that said, "Jim, go back in the house and check her blood sugar level."

I had done this many times in the past, maybe because I am not only obsessive-compulsive but also to assure myself that she would be okay until *she* decided to get up without me forcing her to take her own vitals and go through her medication routine. By this time, she had already slept through the typical morning medication window. She did not think she had missed them in these situations because she always took her night meds so late.

So I went back into the house, grabbed her glucose monitor, and began the test process. My first concern was that she did not budge when I pricked her finger with the small device. My hands were now shaking as I tried to successfully get the drop of blood on the test strip. I nervously waited for the result, only to see a 23 come up on the screen. Thinking that the batteries were low, I checked to see the battery level and then quickly repeated the test. Another 23 popped up. I now tried to wake her up, to no avail. I called 911 feverishly.

(As I type, I now understand why this chapter was so difficult to finish. I had had what I thought was writer's block for about two months.)

I have never been in a room where paramedics have responded to a call for an unconscious subject, but in addition to worrying about whether this was the big event we spoke of together many times, I was also selfishly concerned about what the neighbors would think, or will the medical personnel think that I have been neglectful in her care? A hundred things were flashing across my mind as I was gazing at the seemingly lifeless body of the woman I loved.

I heard the emergency units coming down the street. I opened the wooden door and walked outside to wave them down. They swooped into the house; each one of them had a task they were accomplishing independently, but this was a well-rehearsed team. Again, as I type, I feel myself getting emotional, with tears, as I remember one lady tech slapping her and loudly calling her name. This is the writer's block moment—the one incident that has stayed with me the longest and the strongest. She was slapping the woman I love and screaming at her. They had to ascertain if she could be revived here in our home.

Their first glucose reading was 22, but within a few moments, Mary was now mumbling and then talking, and then she smiled as if recognizing some of the responders but only after she was given an injection. As they began asking her questions to determine her cognitive abilities, the lead person asked me, "Mr. Rioux, tell me what happened, and what did you do first?"

I was embarrassed to reveal that I put some orange juice on her lips, thinking this could begin a process of raising her sugar levels as I awaited the EMT's arrival.

"Mr. Rioux, she could have aspirated!" she seemed to scream.

I will always remember that word. I could have killed her right then, but I told the lady that this was the only thing I knew to do and that I learned it from the movie *Steel Magnolias* when Sally Fields tried to revive Julia Roberts. That comment, made in all seriousness and honesty, only generated what now sounded very much like an even stronger rebuke. But this moment was not the time for me to try to save face. Mary was extremely sick. I almost lost her; she could have died had I not been obedient to the voice of God or one of His ministering angels to go back into the house.

Be still and know that I am God.

—Psalm 46:10 KJV

JAMES, THIS IS BROOKE

As Mary's increasingly sedentary lifestyle continued, with her not wanting to follow through on the exercises that home health nurses were teaching her, the unsteadiness of her legs and feet continued to get worse. As stated before, the calls to neighbors after a fall in my absence were withheld from me by her. I simply did not know how many times these events happened, which explained her familiarity with some of the EMTs. She always had ready-made explanations for bruises on her hands, arms, or legs. Again and again, I was reminded not to worry about her. "I am a grown woman," she would say.

What was also getting worse was her ability to get out of her recliner unassisted. This came to a head on a Monday morning when I was preparing to go to work. She could not get up on her own from the recliner. She had a little difficulty the night before, but she always seemed to rise on her own with some effort, and I just rationalized that the added effort was good for maintaining her muscle tone. But on this morning, she simply could not get up. I absolutely could not leave her, notwithstanding her pleadings not to worry about her. I called my boss and explained; everyone at work was very understanding. Mary and I talked and tried to figure out our next step as I felt overwhelming emotions coming over me.

After a few minutes, I did what I have always done in these situations: go for a ride around the block to think. This is what I would do when writing a school paper or just to clear my head. What happened as I sat in my pickup truck, though, was a new degree of fear that started me audibly crying. *I have finally been broken*, I thought. This had never happened in my life, but there I was in my front yard in my truck, out of Mary's and the neighbors' earshot, crying uncontrollably. I felt completely helpless.

The next moment was another occasion when God called one of His ministering angels into action. The company I work for has always been far different from any other in that moments like these in the life of a truck driver do not go unnoticed or addressed, in this case, immediately.

As I continued to weep, the phone rang, and the caller ID showed an Illinois area code. Word of Mary and our dilemma had gone up the chain quickly.

I answered the call, "James, this is Brooke. How can I help?"

This was the president of the company, ten or fifteen minutes after I had called in. She called to see what she could do to help. It just as well could have been a lower-tier supervisor pushing me on a scenario of my return to work, another "the load must go" type of call. But not today. Brooke wanted to know if I needed a lift chair. She said the charitable arm of the company would pay for it. I had not thought of one of those kinds of chairs. That stopped the emotions from spiraling out of control, and my head was firmly back in its proper place. We chatted for a few minutes, with me promising to call her if necessary.

I went back inside the house and told Mary that I was going to find a lift chair, fighting back more tears generated by the manifestation of a very personal, corporate-level act of human compassion that I had never experienced before. I found a motorized lift chair in Baton Rouge, but because it was a Memorial Day holiday week, the delivery schedule was full. I had to wait for the rain to subside over the next few days and bring the chair home in the back of my pickup myself. By Wednesday, Mary had her lift chair, and once she was on her feet with the slight use of her walker, she was good to go. She told me to go to work. One major hurdle had been cleared, and all was well for about a month or so.

THE FALL

I knew full well of her love for cats, especially the fifteen or twenty that she fed regularly outside that were not ours—feral cats. She had tried to befriend one by force on a previous occasion, but it bit her, resulting in another hospital stay where she almost lost an arm. With the soft heart that she had for animals, I knew to keep her stocked with a large bag of cat food—another form of therapy for her, I thought to a fault.

I had repeatedly "suggested" that she limit her cat feeding chores to the daylight hours. I could tell several more stories that would illustrate how this love for animals was an obsession that she could not rein in for her own good.

A day sometime in early July of 2020, at 2:00 p.m. Michigan time, was a time I vividly remember because I was in the Detroit area, delivering to a chemical plant. I was waiting for my scheduled time to unload. I was leaning on the fender of my trailer, talking with Mary on the phone. I once again mentioned that she should not go out after dark to feed the cats. I expressed to her that she isn't like one of the cats in that she does not have nine lives. I warned her that one night she could fall and that this could be the big one I had always spoken about. She could fall and no one would see her, and she could spend the night on the ground, out of sight and sound of someone to help. I did not talk to her that night. I could not get her on the phone. I figured she was sleeping.

But that night, at some point between eight o'clock and midnight, that very thing happened exactly except for one important detail, and I again give glory to God for His exquisite love and timing. We had a neighbor whose son kept late hours at a frequency that Mary and I had discussed in a less-than-positive manner. "He's always coming in at such late hours," we would murmur to each other.

Well, his habit of keeping late hours was the only reason she survived in this instance. Mary had every intention of going out and feeding the cats at about 8:00 p.m. after dark but never made it; she fell forward out of the front door. The "troubling" late hours of this young man had him getting out of his car at about midnight. As he started toward his house, he heard a faint moaning sound coming from the direction of our home. He walked over to investigate and found Mary on the ground, bleeding from her forehead. It would later be revealed that she had internal bleeding in her brain as well. A night spent on the ground could have very well led to another near-death experience. As bad as this had been, it led to a great regret of mine. I had never laid eyes on this young man before and wanted to hug him and thank him for finding her and saving her life. A few short months later, he lost his own life in an automobile accident. It had to suffice for me that I held his mother after his funeral to express my thanks to her for what he had done for Mary.

For my thoughts are not your thoughts, neither are your ways my ways, saith the Lord.

—Isaiah 55:8 KJV

THEY WERE
WAITING FOR ME

Mary was transported to the local hospital. It was there that they found that she had experienced bleeding in the brain. I suppose that they had given her some form of coagulant to at least control the bleeding to a point where they could transport her to another hospital that was better equipped to handle this type of brain injury. Having made it home from Michigan, I arrived at the hospital just in time for them to tell me that they were about to put her in a Life Flight helicopter to bring her eighty miles south to New Orleans.

The facility there had a unit that specialized in these types of brain injuries, and within a few days, they returned my angel to a bit of normalcy. But this did not happen before a few revealing moments of how the physical and spiritual mind works.

It is not easy to describe or explain these events. I am compelled here to say that in my very humble, unresearched opinion of these types of things, I believe that these moments of seemingly less-than-lucid thoughts should be taken seriously as spiritual events. As described in this section and another to come, these patients are experiencing thoughts and sights that are unexplainable to the witnesses who are present. Mary, in her physically deteriorating condition, had one foot on earth and the other in heaven, which awaited her. She was being prepared for her next "change of status."

While visiting her three or four days after her arrival in New Orleans, she kept stretching her neck to one side while in bed and then asked me if I could move her bed closer to the window. I replied that with all these tubes and wires connected to her, I did not think that would be a wise thing for me to do. Her window gave a long-distance view of Lake Pontchartrain to our south but not from her bed. So I asked her, "Mary, what is it that you want to see?"

She replied, "The clouds. I want to see those beautiful clouds."

"Mary, didn't you see enough clouds on your trip in the helicopter?" I asked.

She then replied with one of those answers that defies our comprehension. "Yes, they were waiting for me."

When I asked what she meant by her answer, all I received back was a slight smile, returning her gaze toward the window and the clouds that she could see. She understood, and even with a feeble attempt to explain to me, she knew what she was seeing and feeling. When you come to think of it, I was the feeble one, years behind her in my comprehension of such matters. This is one of the things, like Habakkuk's witness, that God wanted me to see. I have many more of these yet to come.

This stay in the hospital, caused by the fall, began a period of her confusing the daily events in the hospital as well as phone calls from family with the things that she was watching on television. There were several things that she told me that began my period of being more attentive to the things that she was sharing with me and trying to figure out her thought process, which was like trying to put together a puzzle with missing pieces.

On another day, she seemed a little upset, interspersed with some feelings of joy. She would tell me about long-deceased relatives who came to visit her that day, mostly when the nurses were not present or when I had stepped out. I never once questioned the validity of the events that she was describing. She called the relatives by name and told me what they had discussed. Again, I repeat, this was not the product of her imagination; one would have to know the nature of her spiritual beliefs to understand.

On this day, in a moment when she blended what I believed to be actual spiritual visitations with the current events of the day that she had seen on television, I asked her why she could be a little down with all the "family" coming to see her.

She asked, "Have you seen President Trump around the hospital? He was supposed to come to see me today." This was clearly a product of not being able to separate her experiences from what she was seeing on television. However, the "family visitations"—I believe with all my heart, mind, and soul—were Mary's long-deceased family members' spirits. In my mind, President Trump represented a family member that she dearly loved who had not visited her in spirit, and she was disappointed.

After less than two weeks, Mary was on the mend but was transported to the first of a series of physical rehabilitation facilities in the Baton Rouge area. The intent was to attempt to get her leg strength back to the point where she could live a normal life in her less-than-ideal condition. She was in temporary residence at several of these facilities over the next few months. It became noticeably clear to me, however, that the time was quickly approaching when we would have to consider the reality of a full-time stay at a nursing home. She simply could not take care of herself at home in the long term, and the insurance would not pay for twenty-four-hour home care. Because of our financial condition, retiring early to take care of her was out of the question.

It also became noticeably clear that she would have no part of a nursing home. Though I had always been true to our marriage vows, she thought that I was sending her away, throwing away the keys, and that she would never see me again. This absolutely was not the case. I visited her as regularly as the new COVID-19 restrictions would allow me.

At one point, sometime in the fall of 2020, during one of the rehab stays, they noticed her breathing becoming labored because of her fluid retention. At first, they treated her for pneumonia, but with no relief. Her condition became critical, and because of the limited capabilities of this rehab facility, it was decided that she was to be taken down the street to a hospital to determine the cause of her fluid retention. This was the point at which they found that she had reduced kidney function. Remember, as stated earlier, I was told by an alternative medicine professional about five years earlier that if she continued taking the now-more-than-twenty medications, this exact thing would be the consequence. The human body simply cannot filter out the toxicity and heavy metals contained in prescription drugs, especially in the quantities that she was taking.

Once she went back home, a catheter was used to drain her kidneys with home health nurses coming in regularly. This, however, was just not enough for her to be considered "responsible" enough to care for herself, especially considering her history of not doing so in the past with her diabetes. She was not following through with breathing and lightweight exercises that she was left to do on her own. As a result, about a week before Thanksgiving 2020, with her strength waning, we were once again in the hospital with her spiraling health, worsened now by her poorly performing kidneys.

While there, she was still adamant about taking care of herself at home and refused to agree to go to a nursing home. I was only her husband and did not have the legal authority to have her admitted to such a facility against her wishes without the intervention of a court. In fact, we had just finished having the nursing home conversation when a couple of ladies from the hospital's physical therapy department walked in. This was not exercise time; they were there to have her demonstrate her ability to get out of bed on her own power. After a couple of attempts, it was clear that she was not able to do so. The therapists were there at the behest of the palliative doctor. He later described himself as an end-of-life specialist, his responsibility being to provide access at his direction to the care and facilities that would make her as safe and comfortable as possible in her final days.

Though I knew that Mary's situation was dire, this palliative doctor was the first to use the terminology "end-of-life care." After making his diagnostic observations, he sat on the couch with me and explained his purpose. His manner of speaking had a very calming effect. Like in my conversation with Brooke, I had never been treated in such a kind and informative manner by a doctor until this.

I had not heard of palliative care prior to this moment, but a few minutes later, in his capacity, after having witnessed for himself that Mary could not stand on her own, his decision had been made. When he saw that lack of ability, he was very direct but sensitive when he looked at her and told her, "Well, girl, looks like you are ready for a twenty-four-hour care facility."

He told her that it was his call to make and that he could not see her going home and taking care of herself to any degree. She never lost eye contact with him. She even had a slight smile on her face.

And then, the woman I love, the same one who an hour earlier was still completely opposed to going to a nursing home, steadfastly responded, "I agree," without once looking at me. And that was that. She began what would be her next-to-last trip to a nursing facility. On Thanksgiving Day, 2020, I was profoundly grateful that she would get the kind of care that I could not provide at our home—the care that she needed and deserved.

A NEW HOME

What began as a new sense of hope for Mary quickly escalated into a very cruel and demeaning period of separation of sorts. The COVID-19 restrictions had arrived in what, to me, felt like a Nazi regime takeover. I will not elaborate on this to any degree more than to describe it as "man's inhumanity to man" and that God has a way of settling the score for these types of offenses.

This atmosphere having been addressed, my visitations at first were restricted to outside meetings, six feet apart, in masks even in the fresh air environs, set by appointment only, with two grown adults being watched over like children at a daycare center. As a couple, especially with her diagnosed depression, we were accustomed to hugs—a thirty-second hug to be exact. Experts suggest that a thirty-second hug "releases the feel-good hormone oxytocin which creates a stronger bond and connection between the huggers." Well, this habit was a thing of the past for us, which is one thing that stole her smile from me. It even subjected her to strong, cold winds in January. That one, like many other COVID-19 restrictions, defied logic without any reasonable alternatives forthcoming.

Eventually, things eased up, and I was allowed to see her in her assigned room, but only after a COVID-19 test before each visit. This return to intimacy, if one could call it that, had me being met with a joyful smile, which caused a significant improvement in her emotional and spiritual well-being, including mine. When I was out on the road having a difficult day, all I had to do was call her and hear her voice, and then I would feel that all was right with the world for me. But there we were, out of the presence of the nursing staff, with returning hugs as well as prayers together while holding hands.

In this setting, I was now introduced to hospice professionals. This facility did not have an in-house hospice. I even hesitate to call them nurses. Their job is a higher calling, one with a spiritual connection.

One such specialized nurse from a hospice facility in Baton Rouge visited during the week, aptly and beautifully named The Crossing. I learned so much from this special angel of God. Hospice work is truly more than a job. I am sure their days became hectic and tiresome going home to family, just like everyone else's. The higher rewards for them come during moments that a "mere mortal" cannot comprehend. Yes, I put them on just such a pedestal.

This lady, Katy by name, showed me that she was there not only to contribute to and monitor Mary's care but also to answer questions for me that the nursing staff could not. The only limit to the answers she gave me was my curiosity. Because she had been involved with end-of-life care for several years, her replies to me seemed to be emotionally exclusive to our situation. I saw her listening to me with direct eye contact, like she was looking into my soul and, by association, into Mary's.

With ever-decreasing kidney function, which meant a minimal water intake, her medications were limited to the ones that could be given by injection or by drip bag. There was a DNR order in place—do not resuscitate. This meant they were making her as comfortable as possible while she was able to consume what little food she could. I visited as often as I was allowed now that she was in her own private room. We spoke to each other up until the point when her speech was nothing more than a mumble. I did not force the issue; these were sweet moments, just being in each other's presence. I felt it a privilege to have been selected by God twenty years prior to being her spouse and allowed to be a witness to those sacred moments.

Through all those last months, there was never a question in my mind as to whether she knew that the end was near. Her facial countenance changed—not a sense of hopelessness; it was more peaceful, very unlike the stoic look in her face and eyes during the outside visits or the brief period when she was in a semi-private room.

When she could still speak well enough to be understood, she started asking what I think of as "the question." She kept asking me about the other place that she was going to and would get a little sideways with me when I did not answer to her satisfaction. She was not speaking of heaven, for she knew that no one was privy to that information—only God knew.

So what was this other place she spoke of? Then Katy, the visiting hospice nurse, pulled me outside one day and asked me, "Mr. Rioux, have you told her that she was going to another facility after this one?"

I replied that I had not and told her that Mary had been asking me the same question. Katy said that she had quizzed the staff at the nursing home about the matter, and no one there had spoken of it. She told me that, given her condition at that point, the doctor had no plan to move her to a stand-alone hospice facility.

But as it is written: "Eye hath not seen, nor ear heard, nor has entered into the heart of man, the things which God has prepared for those who love Him."'

—1 Corinthians 2:9 KJV

THE GIFT

It was Friday, April 23, 2021. Mary understood that things were coming to her earthly sojourn's conclusion. The room was emotionally still, as she was then only able to mumble to me. Her body was so sacred to me. I almost hesitated to even touch my wife of twenty years. It was as though her room was an edifice, acting as a portal for what was yet to come. I gently slipped my hand and then my arm under her neck so that I could softly rest her head there. I pressed my cheek against her forehead so that I could hear her audible mumbles. Since moving into her private room, she did not complain even once and never asked for food or water; she just smiled or seemed very content, at the very least.

I would tell her stories or sing her favorite hymns. She would respond with a smile or try to sing or hum along with me. Sometimes I would just stand there, absorbing the peace that she had filled the air with. I was no longer worrying about the nurses walking in; they knew that the time was close.

Katy, the visiting hospice nurse, walked in and looked at Mary as lovingly as I have. She whispered to me, "Mr. Rioux, we really cannot explain what is keeping her going. She has not had food for some time now since she has lost the ability to swallow. She has not been given water for several days for fear she would aspirate; they have just been wetting her lips to keep them from drying out and cracking. The human body can go for forty days without water. We just do not know why she is holding on. As best as we can understand, we think that she has been waiting on someone or something to occur, as do many people in her condition."

I told Katy that Mary understood her daughter's absence—a mother of two, nine hundred miles away. She knew it would be a hardship for her to be there. She was always so proud of Karen and all that she had accomplished in her life under difficult circumstances. She would prefer that Karen remain in North Carolina and care for her grandsons.

Katy's visit concluded. I soon left and returned the next two days, Saturday and Sunday. I spent the better part of those days with her. When I left Friday, though, she was very aware of my presence, chatting with me as it were, having been reduced to mumbles.

When I returned Saturday morning, though, she heard me come in. She looked my way and returned to what she was "doing." This morning, she seemed fidgety, making what at the time seemed like jerking motions. Katy called it terminal agitation. I came to her side, kissed her, and told her, "Good morning, my angel," the nickname she loved me to call her. She looked my way, gave me a look as if to say, "I'm busy right now," and then returned to whatever she was "doing." Mary was far from agitated. What she was involved with took me the better part of a day and a half to figure out. She obviously felt that she had some work yet to complete before her own "crossing." Her activities seemed to transcend my presence in the room, even on this side of the veil. She was smiling and laughing.

Sunday afternoon, I started to understand that she was mouthing her conversations with someone on the wall and with someone in her lap. She had a look of immense joy on her face. Her beautiful blue eyes were very much alive with energy. She was as active and "talkative" as she had been in weeks, just not with me. All I could do was just watch in amazement and awe.

It was on Sunday that I came to my senses as I was made to recall her absolute knowledge of the penultimate family reunion that awaited her on the other side of the veil. Indeed, she had one foot there already, the other one lingering here for whatever reason she felt that she had required herself to stay for just a little longer.

What was she doing those two days?

She was conversing and interacting with the attendees of that grand and glorious welcome committee in the heavens. I saw her eyes darting back and forth up near the ceiling on the wall to her right and directly ahead as she was looking at each one there, attempting to move her arms in response to her words. Her face was "beaming as brightly as the noonday sun," a reference she would understand.

But what of the person in her lap? Mary was baby talking to a child in her lap, and then I remembered that she had lost a child during the initial stages of pregnancy years ago, after Karen's birth. This was the spiritual representation of that child sitting on her lap; the difference in expression and demeanor in how she interacted in that direction made me certain of its truth.

Part one of what Katy had related to me was occurring before my eyes. In a statement of declaration on behalf of my wife and myself, I knew with certainty that her family had come for her; they were calling Mary Elisabeth home.

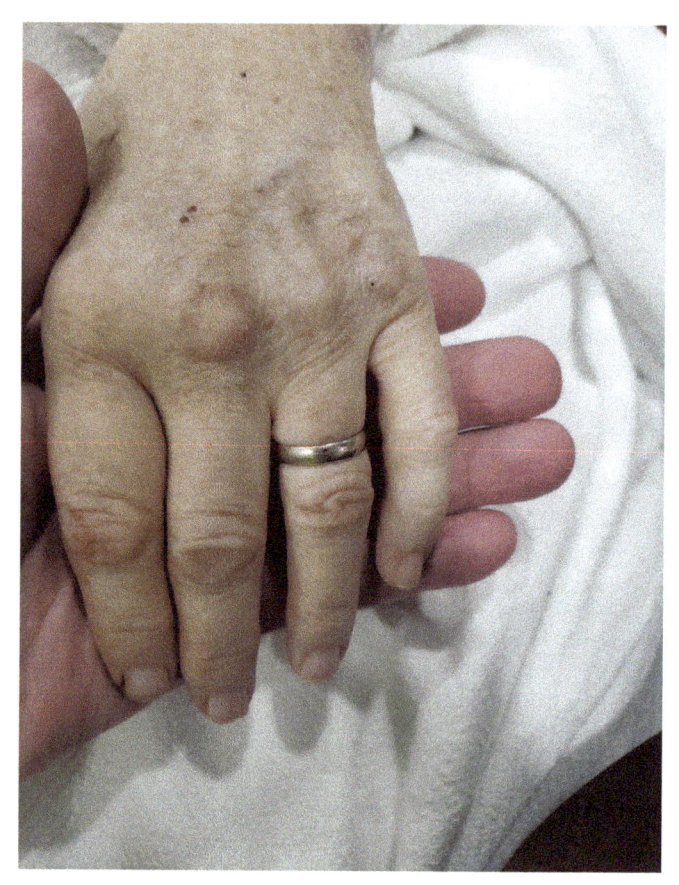

THE BLESSING

The next morning, Monday, began on an extremely negative note as I was called into the administrator's office. I referred to her in that manner because no one referred to her by name. They referred to her as the administrator, and she introduced herself only as the administrator. I was strongly rebuked for spending such an exorbitant amount of time with my wife over the weekend, who was just days or even hours away from drawing her last breath. Her clear intent was to have me grovel and beg for an extended period of visitation; the established but unknown to me time limit was thirty minutes.

Thirty minutes as each of her heart beats were mysterious in that I did not know if it would be her last. Thirty minutes for a woman I called every day over the past twenty years, thirty minutes with someone who I spent every available hour with. Thirty minutes as she was perched in bed with one foot here and the other at a family reunion called in her honor.

I would not beg or grovel with the administrator, who was clearly on an ego trip and completely devoid of compassion of any degree. "Thirty minutes it will be, ma'am," as I also went into a bit of a diatribe on the current events in play here at this moment on a global scale, but that I would not allow stealing the joy of the previous days or the thirty-minute visit about to transpire. I turned and left for Mary's room.

As I walked in, I checked the time, kissed my wife's forehead, and slipped my arm under her head as I was accustomed to doing. I felt a sense of urgency.

"Mary." I spoke softly to her. She knew. She knew why I was there on that day. She had to know. Extraordinary gifts accompany those in this condition as many other abilities have withered away.

Somehow, by some spiritual power, I also knew why I was there on that day.

"Mary, you know it's time."

She quickly nodded in approval, with an accompanying smile. She knew, and I knew.

"Mary, do you want a blessing?"

Again, she swiftly nodded her head in approval, like my mother many years earlier.

I knew the time was close, so I wore a coat and tie, standing before her. I placed my hands on her head and began, "Mary Elisabeth Rioux, by the power vested in me—" The words that I cannot begin to remember flowed from the heavens through me as one of God's humble servants. It continued for some time as my hands almost seemed to vibrate upon her head; the spirit in the room was so sweet and strong.

I concluded the blessing in the name of Jesus Christ and said amen. Any family member of hers knew that at the conclusion of any prayer, Mary had better hear those present say amen, or it was as if they had never said it. I waited for her amen in reply—even a mumble. I repeated it louder, "Amen!" Still, I received no reply from my angel. A bit worried, I opened my eyes, only to see her still beautiful red lips puckered up for a kiss, her only way at that point of communicating her concluding amen to me. This was the most memorable kiss we had ever shared, for it would prove to be our last. I was experiencing the affectations of a person who was halfway home.

Oh, they tell me of a cloudless day
Oh. the land of a cloudless sky,
Oh, they tell me of home where
no storm clouds rise
Oh, they tell me of an unclouded day.

—"Uncloudy Day" written
by Willie Nelson

THE OTHER PLACE

The following Friday, just four days later, there seemed to have been a tug-of-war for Mary between the administration of the nursing facility and the newly made decision by her attending physician to move her. It certainly was not at the behest of Mary, for by that time, she was unable to communicate her desire for a move. I was certainly not consulted.

Someone during this very hazy time said that this happened later Friday afternoon or early evening and that the administrator got involved and returned to the facility. I was made to understand that things got ugly. My best efforts to remember how I came to be aware of all of this escaped me, and I had—and still do—put it out of my mind.

I was determined not to let outside forces diminish the sheer beauty of God's presence manifested through His actions in these last moments of Mary's appointed earthly status. These were sacred moments. This tug-of-war involving the evil one, literally for Mary's body, was just the first, but not the last, demonstration of man's inhumanity to man.

Let me pause here briefly to rightly credit the poet Robert Burns for having said, "Man's inhumanity to man makes countless thousands mourn."

And then I likewise credit South African poet Alan Paton's antidote to such behavior when he said, "There is only one way in which one can endure man's inhumanity to man and that is to try, in one's own life, to exemplify man's humanity to man."

These moments had to be addressed here for my grandchildren, to whom I dedicate this book, for them to know that even during the most spirit-filled days of our lives, evil awaits in the dark corridors.

For reasons unknown to me, Mary's doctor called an audible at some point on Friday to move her. I was informed either Friday night or early Saturday morning. Anyone associated with hospice care involved in this process had my trust. What they said was the right thing to do.

I was told that the move would be made in the late morning hours. I assumed that she would be in this "other place" somewhere between noon and two on Saturday afternoon. I arrived back home from the road Friday night, and while the move was in progress and Mary was being made comfortable, I decided to allow things to simmer down there while I did some things around our home.

I started cutting the grass and told myself that I would go inside at about five-thirty to take a shower and go sit with her at The Crossing, the other place that she had been asking about for a few weeks. Again, God was in the inner workings of this entire season of Mary's life. He knew her desire, and He made it happen. God, the doctor, and Katy had her back.

I finished cutting grass a little early and had just sat down when my phone rang. It was 5:25 p.m.

"Mr. Rioux, this is the nurse at The Crossing Hospice. Mary's breathing has become labored, and you might want to come on up here. This is generally a sign that her time is at hand. Take your time, drive safely, no rush. We will see you in a little bit."

I cannot explain the peace that came over me. Give the glory to God. I did not panic. I quickly took a shower, put on my suit, and drove the speed limit the entire twenty-six miles to see Mary. To this day, I have zero comprehension of how I walked into that building at 6:00 p.m., just thirty-five minutes after I sat down at home.

I walked through the front door to a long, circular hallway back to the after-hours nurse's station. There I was met by three ladies behind the counter, one of whom I knew, Tracy, from church. We locked eyes as she cocked her head to one side as if confused and said, "Hi, Brother Rioux." Another lady closest to the door spoke to me as she met me at the beginning of the hallway that led to the patient rooms. She caught up to me and placed her right arm through my left arm, as a couple would do. She began to speak, but because I wore hearing aids and my left side was my worst side, I told her, "If you want me to hear you, you are going to have to get on my right side."

As I continued to walk, she had to run behind me to wrap her left arm around my right arm. Again, I continued to walk until she said loudly, "Mr. Rioux, STOP!"

I stopped and turned to the nurse. We were then facing each other.

She said, "She's gone. She passed a few minutes ago."

I later learned she passed away at 5:40 p.m.

I was then frozen in my tracks. In a voice as if from an angel, she very sweetly told me of Mary's crossing. I cannot remember her name, but I can find the spot where she communicated to me the beginning of my angel's family reunion with her mother, father, her beloved granny, Uncle Charles, and all the rest who were calling her home the weekend prior.

The nurse was still clinging to me, explaining the things that were to transpire over the next hour or so as she brought me into Mary's room, which was hers for all of six hours. I turned, and the angelic nurse was gone. I called my daughter Jessica to come. My daughter Annie with three young children was unable to come. I called Mary's daughter and sister in North Carolina and then gave Mary a parting blessing after Jessica's arrival.

Even in death, with a towel folded under her neck, she was so beautiful. That she was radiating with a glow is not an overstatement. She made it to the "other place" she asked Katy and me about. She knew. She knew. She was a North Carolina Tar Heel, and she knew what she wanted and received her wish.

The coroner's office arrived to retrieve Mary. I thought, *She is no longer here. She has risen*, a verse borrowed from Matthew 28:6. But still, the attendants were so gentle, as if her soul were still present. Jessica and I just gazed at each other as she was wheeled out. We followed them down the hall. We stopped at the nurse's station to thank them.

My rock, Jessica and I, just looked at each other as if to ask, "What now, with Mary's long earthly journey having concluded?" I could see in her eyes that she did not want me to just go home, so we went to Coffee Call and ate some beignets. I was doing a lot of talking and saying nothing, though I was speaking actual words. I was in a daze. After my turn to settle down, I felt good enough to drive safely home. I have often questioned what people mean when they say he or she "was there for me." On this night, I understood what it meant for someone to be there for me.

Mary Elisabeth Rioux passed away at 5:40 p.m., Saturday, May 1, 2021. I had missed her departure by twenty minutes. I have never, for a moment, questioned God's decision to send her home when He did without my presence. Somehow, I understood that this was appropriate.

For so many years, when someone has lost a member of the family, I just leave the words of comfort with them that are found in this hospice poem by Henry van Dyke. I thought of this as Jessica and I stood there.

> *I am standing upon the seashore. A ship, at my side, spreads her white sails to the moving breeze and starts for the blue ocean. She is an object of beauty and strength. I stand and watch her until, at length, she hangs like a speck of white cloud just where the sea and sky come to mingle with each other*
>
> *Then, someone at my side says,*
> *"There, she is gone."*
> *Gone where?*
> *Gone from my sight. That is all. She is just as large in mast, hull and spar as she was when she left my side. And, she is just as able to bear her load of living freight to her destined port.*
> *Her diminished size is in me—not in her.*
> *And, just at the moment when someone says, "There, she is gone," there are other eyes watching her coming, and other voices ready to take up the glad shout,*
> *"Here she comes!"*
> *And that is dying...*

WITHIN 48 HOURS

Mary's last week of mortality was far different from what I had ever expected losing a loved one might feel like. If her death were because of an unexpected medical occurrence or an accident, it would have been far different. My father died suddenly of a massive heart attack in 1987, after not having experienced sickness his entire life.

Mary's premature passing was expected for many years, even before her first foot surgery a few years prior. As much as others and I had encouraged her to make better decisions, her path was chosen, and the manner of her death was set. Though she was the one to suffer the pain in her many episodes over the years, her family and I were left with the emotional pain of our premature loss for many years to come.

During the last week though, she was not feeling any of that. She was preparing for and subsequently drawing her last breaths in an atmosphere of peaceful contentment. She arrived at the "other place," where she knew that she was supposed to be. Six hours later, she slipped away from us into the arms of her granny and others beyond an uncloudy sky.

Oh, how splendid things would be if our grand and glorious days were never followed by the cruel and unexpected *however* of life. How wonderful it would have been if the beautiful events of Saturday were not followed by the revelation of an unfortunate and costly clerical error concerning her life insurance and the following story of the visit of another of "man's inhumanity to man."

On the Monday after her death, I called to inquire about beginning the process for the payment of her death benefit. I was quickly made to understand that the policy was simply not in place. I could not produce documentation of what I thought were the properly coded payroll deduction payments. A corporate merger was involved, and I have since learned that this very thing is far more common than it should be for these types of transactions. The bottom line was that the policy was not active, and I could not prove otherwise. The outcome, though, was that later, the same charitable arm of the company that offered to pay for a lift chair for Mary two years earlier would step in and help pay for Mary's cremation.

I still had an appointment that was set for Monday afternoon with the funeral service company. Monday had not started on a good note; my blood pressure was already high and was about to get worse. My daughter Jessica had left her workplace to meet me at the funeral home but went to another company address and never made it to ours. So I went through the process with this young female representative alone. She tried several times to upsell me on some services, but the bottom line was that I had an extremely strict amount of money to work with, and we ended up with the most basic plan available. I had no indication from this young lady of the series of phone calls that were to transpire, as she desperately attempted to upsell me again on the phone while I was going home. All of this happened within forty-eight hours of Mary's death.

The upsell was based on a supposed COVID-19 mandate issued by the governor, stating that even though Mary was to be cremated, she would still have to be embalmed. There were a couple more that she mentioned that were going to increase my cash outlay—cash I did not have. By the time I got home, I was fuming. When my blood pressure increased because of the anger created by this circumstance, I could feel it. Once I arrived home, I pulled my emotions together, but still, my blood pressure was 160/120. I simply could not go on without some serious meditation so I could calm down. With a blood pressure reading that high, God certainly intervened and preserved me.

It was still only 4:00 p.m., still less than forty-eight hours after Mary's eyes closed forever, so I googled the state's COVID-19 mandates and was able to ascertain on my own that no such mandates had been enacted. In fact, I found a site with all the state's COVID-19-related mandates, and there were none concerning cremations. I then picked up the phone and called the state's regulatory board for funeral directors and services.

A nice lady answered the phone, and after relating my story to her, she said that she had just gotten off the phone with the same young lady who was asking questions about those mandates only to have to tell her that they did not exist. An argument ensued with the young lady hanging up in frustration. The representative with this state board then told me, "Mr. Rioux, I suggest you call a lawyer."

A few weeks later, I called a few lawyers and wasn't able to find one who was willing to take the case. At the moment, planning a memorial service for my wife was my priority. But this young lady and the owner were not through with their upsell attempts.

In our church, there was a beautiful ceremony that involved three ladies who were to dress the deceased in proper ceremonial burial garments, even for cremation. The three ladies who were especially close to Mary were called, and an appointment was set for them to perform this ceremony on Wednesday. The crematory was forty miles south of our hometown, but upon arriving at the facility, the ladies were told that they could only watch from afar, which was not acceptable. After some phone calls with me back and forth, it was decided that they could perform the ceremony themselves but only after purchasing some Hazmat-type personal protection suits, again, according to the nonexistent gubernatorial mandates.

When the owner realized that this continued subterfuge was not working, he angrily called me and stated that I had thirty minutes to tell him where to send my wife's body, or he would bring her to the morgue. I quickly made a phone call and gave him the address of an alternative site. The three friends of Mary just barely arrived at the other facility before the hearse and the alternative funeral home representative arrived. Evildoers had now reared their ugly heads three times within five days. The cremation was accomplished at twice the cost because it had to be contracted to another crematory.

These types of ugly behaviors crop up every now and then, and it took me a great deal of time to decide whether to include them here, but again, if I have dedicated this book to my grandchildren, they will benefit one day in some way for having been exposed to the sweet and beautiful stories of life—as well as the ugly. The first outweighs the latter and tempers the pain.

The proper ceremony was performed by these special ladies for their friend, and she was cremated. The following Saturday, a beautiful and special memorial service was conducted with Mary's daughter and family in attendance from North Carolina.

In the day of prosperity be happy, but in the day of adversity consider—God has made the one as well as the other.

—Ecclesiastes 7:14 KJV

THE CARD

There never seems to be a closing chapter in a relationship like ours. Every ending is just a change of status, a new beginning in this story for Mary and me. But our lives spent together for twenty years had a surprising but welcoming postscript to come after the conclusion of her life and all the formalities mentioned above.

After the many "thinking rides" without a real destination, quiet nights spent alone, and the Christmas holiday, at some point in early January, I received a card in the mail. It was not out of the ordinary among the many other ones that we receive during the holidays.

I glanced at the return address, but it did not immediately ring a bell. Upon opening the envelope, though, I instantly remembered the name. This was from Tracy, the lady from church who was behind the counter at the nurse's station the night Mary died, the one who called me by name but with a confused look on her face, a look that this card explained. It was a tender mercy of the Lord that was made possible only because another nurse had brought me back to Mary's room at The Crossing and not her through a card received eight months later.

It read as follows,

Dear Brother Rioux,

I just wanted you to know that I have attempted to write this letter several times, each time having a lack of words to say. I am a nurse that works at Clarity Hospice (The Crossing) occasionally, and I just happened to be working the night your precious wife passed. I was not her assigned nurse that day, but I knew her time was short, so I was sitting in her room with her until you were able to come. I did not know at the time that she was your wife, it wasn't until you came that I made the connection.

But the reason I felt prompted to write this letter is to tell you that I was with her when she passed. I held her hand and told her that it was okay for her to go home and that Jesus was waiting for her. I didn't know that she was a member of the church, but there was a sweet spirit that filled the room and a feeling of such peace. And I just wanted you to know that she wasn't alone, and that her passing was peaceful, and she looked so calm and without any distress, and I just thought that you might want to know that.

I pray that you had a nice holiday season and that you felt the comfort and peace that only the Lord can give.

Much love,
Tracy

This letter serves as a testament to the extraordinary gifts of hospice professionals. If one were to read this letter again, it would be quite easy to spot the hand of God in many of the circumstances surrounding Tracy's presence there on this sacred and solemn night.

I called her upon receipt of this card, and she said she typically did not work on weekends, but something told her to go when called. She volunteered to sit with Mary when no one was immediately assigned to her. She could have just sat there with her, catching up on paperwork, but she held her hand and spoke to her. In doing these things, she comforted Mary, escorting her to the veil. She also comforted me and her daughter, to whom I gave this card. She also told me that many patients in this condition are not as calm as Mary was. They seem to be fighting the process of dying.

The three things that she told me that will remain with me forever were that (1) she was not alone, (2) she was calm, and then this: (3) "Brother Rioux, she knew where she was going."

Oh, how we cried the day you left us
We gathered 'round your grave to grieve
Wish I could see the angels faces
When they hear your sweet voice sing

Go rest high on that mountain
Son your work on earth is done
Go to heaven a-shoutin'
Love for the Father and the Son

> "Go Rest High on That Mountain"
> —Songwriter Vincent Grant Gill

REST HIGH ON YOUR MOUNTAIN

As the weeks and months passed after Mary's memorial service, I had a feeling of being lost, not knowing what to do during my days off. Working has always been my antidote; it is all I have ever known to do—go back to work. When I get more than three days off, I get nervous. When I was at home, though, I could not sit still for awfully long. I had gotten rid of the television; nothing interested me. I would just sit and stare and wonder, *What's next?* Then there was the old standby solution: I would get in my truck and go for a ride. Just drive, not knowing where to go, just point it in any direction and see where I end up.

After four or five expeditions of trying to outlast my uncertainty and outrun my loneliness, I seemed to end up close to one location every time—the nursing home. It was not intentional. I knew she was not there any longer, but it was all I had done for six months—just drive thirty-six miles to see her.

But there was one thing I was certain I had to do, and that was to bring Mary's earthly remains to her final earthly home. I would bring her ashes home to the one place where she would want her remains to spend eternity, under the circumstances: the Smoky Mountains, the North Carolina side of those beautiful Cherokee hills. She would have never approved of cremation, but I had no choice. Her sister certainly did not want it that way, but this was the circumstance I found myself in.

It took me some time and courage to break the news to my daughters that an impromptu road trip was in the offing. I waited for the right time when I had extracted work and co-parenting schedules from the two of them. The necessary and meaningful trip was done in a very, very spur-of-the-moment way. I called Mary's daughter in North Carolina and asked her if they would be home the Saturday after Thanksgiving (2021). I made that call the Saturday before Thanksgiving. She replied with a confused-sounding yes. I then asked what I needed to bring from our house that belonged to her mother. She named a few things, after which I said that I was prepared to bring her the sewing machine that belonged to her great-grandmother, Mary's beloved granny. I then invited them to come and join us as we spread her mother's ashes in the Smoky Mountains, four hundred miles from her home, which she understandably declined.

With these hastily prepared plans made, my two daughters, Mary's ashes, a 1920s-something White rotary special sewing machine in a wooden cabinet, and I set out in Mary's van for the nine-hundred-mile trip on Thursday night, straight through, nothing silly like hotel stays; we had things to do. We made it to Mary's daughter's house at about 3:00 p.m. on Friday, unloaded the van, distributed hugs, gave her teenage grandsons an unplanned talk about how much their granny loved them and expected of them, and took off.

The next stop was six hours northwest to the Appalachian Foothills town of Dillsboro, North Carolina, just short of the Smoky Mountain National Park gateway town of Cherokee. We arrived at about 2:00 a.m. Exhausted, we first checked out the balcony from our third-floor room, which overlooked a briskly flowing creek that seemed to dance over the rocks below, illuminated by an almost full moon. Annie, my thirty-two-year-old daughter, who, like her sister and dad, had never stayed in a $350 a night room before, was the first to walk out and then excitedly popped her head back inside and said something I will never forget: "Dad, there's a real live creek down there." Precious and priceless moment!

After driving roughly 1,300 miles in twenty-four hours, we slept in these high-dollar digs for all of five hours, ate the continental breakfast downstairs, and were off to take a stroll and discover a few souvenirs the fifteen winding miles away in Cherokee, something Mary would have done for sure.

We took our time in town and drifted our separate ways after having been in the van, breathing the same air for so long. We just took the time to unwind before we drove the four thousand-foot elevation and climbed to the top of "Ole Smoky" to do what we truly came to Appalachia to do.

It cannot be overstated how much she loved this area. She grew up in Goldsboro, North Carolina, about 350 miles back in the eastern part of the state, and an hour and a half drive north of where her daughter now lived. Mary's father was a police officer and always saw to it that the family was afforded yearly trips that he meticulously prepared for. There scarcely seemed to be a destination in America that her father hadn't taken them to. She was so proud of him and staunchly defended his character and integrity.

Mary wanted us to do the same as we shared our life together. She always wanted to take me to Gatlinburg, especially to The Apple Barn and Cider Mill in Sevierville on the other side of this mountain. We never made it to the places that we wanted to travel to because of her health issues. But in late November of 2022, my two girls and I spent the same time of the year as we did in 2021, but in Sevierville. Quite by accident, as we rounded a turn, there it was—The Apple Barn. I froze, slowed down, and explained myself to my daughters.

"Daddy, do you want to stop and go in?"

"No," I replied. "Maybe next year."

Our home was filled with numerous items covered in apples: dinnerware, glasses, cups, aprons, and notepads.

But on this morning in 2021, as our ascent up the mountain began, my mood changed as all these thoughts concerning the things that she loved flooded my mind. Airplane rides; all furry creatures; her homemade biscuits; the way she cut her spaghetti noodles before eating, just like her dad; sewing, but never on a Sunday, for she would quote her Granny, "Never sew on a Sunday because you will have to rip out all of those stitches when you get to heaven"; her office supply fetish; and many other memories became a torrent of emotions.

THE CLIMB

We were almost at the peak; our Google Maps was useless, as we had lost our phone signal five miles behind us. I had been watching carefully to be certain that the spot I had chosen to perform this brief ceremony was on the North Carolina side of the mountain. Alas, I found the spot, a small pull-off concrete area with a not-too-steep open-air slope to a boulder about fifty feet away that I could perch my foot on to keep my balance.

I immediately felt God's presence at this spot, as one does throughout these peaks and valleys, but I felt it especially strong here. My daughters were not as convinced when I took a step sideways as I straddled the decline. "Daddy!" I took another sidestep. "Daddy, be careful!" In unison, they shouted louder the farther down I went, "DADDY, no! Be careful, Daddy!" I was sixty-four at the time, but God was at my side, urging me further. I felt that I was protected by His love and my sense of purpose, knowing that He would catch me if I fell. But alas, I reached the boulder safely and on two feet, thanks in part to the excellent "coaching" from the parking area above. Not that they did not want to come down the mountain with me. Annie Rebecca and Jessica Marie, in an act of love, allowed me to do this alone—a last private moment with Mary.

After catching my breath, I looked around me as I captured a once-in-a-lifetime view from down the side of this awe-inspiring mountain. I took a few deep breaths, feeling as if they energized my entire being. I retrieved the bag of her sweet remains from the box, cradled her in my left arm, and then raised my arm to the square. I then began, "By the power vested in me, I consecrate these hills and valleys, with their flowers and grasses, caressed by these Cherokee winds, as the final resting place for the cremains of Mary Elisabeth

Percise Rioux. That they shall remain in these mountains that she loved, in the state of her birth, forever and ever, and this I say, in the name of Jesus Christ, amen." I then cast her ashes to the wind to begin her new ministry.

For the first time in twenty years, I said a prayer, a blessing, in her presence, knowing that I would not physically hear her *amen* in reply. But I felt her as her sweet spirit echoed, gently sweeping down to the valley floor, past the trees, bushes, flowers, and animals that awaited her arrival, just as her granny had awaited her spirit in the heavenly family reunion. Indeed, this was her final resting place; not just this spot but the entire Appalachian region would be her new earthly home. She will not rest; she will not be held down in one exact spot. Independent as she was, she will dance upon this land forever with the Cherokees that came before her.

As these thoughts raced through my mind, very unexpectedly, I began to cry out, with more of a bellowing sound, in loving agony over the loss of my dear, sweet Mary. "My angel!" It echoed and vibrated through the air and seemed at length to boomerang back to me, urging me to turn around and climb back up that mountain. I obeyed, and as I spun around, a power that I cannot begin to describe pushed me back up that mountain, never a misstep, assisted by the returning shouts of, "Daddy, be careful! Daddy, slow down! Daddy, Daddy, DADDY."

Upon arriving at the top, I then collapsed into the arms of one of my daughters and cried some more. But once the sobbing ceased, I felt the same spirit that urged me down and then back up the hill begin to urge me back to the van and across the top of the Smoky Mountains into Tennessee. Mary was once again totally at peace, and my life lay ahead of me. Though I felt for a time that I had left her behind, I could almost hear her whisper from amidst the cool November breeze, "You go now, darling. Do something great and wonderful for the rest of your life. I know you will. I have work to do here. Go now."

So I did as she implored me to do, not just at this moment, but at many points throughout our marriage. She had just blessed my future with her sweet, loving blessing.

Then we departed, with Tennessee in our view through the windshield of Mary's van.

*And God shall wipe away all their tears
from their eyes; and there shall be no
more death, neither sorrow, nor crying,
neither shall there be any more pain: for
the former things are passed away.*

—Revelation 21:4 KJV

Much love,
—Paw Paw

*There isn't a story that we can
tell better than our own.*

—James Matthew Rioux

AFTERTHOUGHTS

For my grandchildren: Madelyn, Lucas, Owen, Kenli, Camille, and Cannon

We began with stories, and we will end with stories. After all, "the call" that propelled an idea into an actual book was the reminder that it would be about my stories. I had never considered that I might have the kind of stories sufficiently intriguing to include in an offering such as this. Jessica and Annie knew. God knew.

There was a time that I belonged to a church that asked me to travel to other local units to speak at their services. There was a leader who gave great talks that included wonderful stories. I thought that I just did not have the kind of stories that could hold the attention of folks for any length of time. Then the "still, small voice" would show me connections between the subject matter and things that I had experienced in my life. A theme that is demonstrated throughout this book is applied here, as God was preparing the talk in my mind that He wanted me to give. He was preparing the congregation to hear His talk, not mine.

These whisperings always appeared as I was finishing a talk for an upcoming Sunday and already had a set of bullet points of what I thought would work. Then at that point, usually on the night before an appointed talk the next morning, God would flood my mind with stories. At first, I would resist the urge to change what I had already prepared until He made me realize that I had tried to do it on my own.

I always began my talk with my background, which included telling them that I was a truck driver. On one particular Sunday, as others were walking up and thanking me for coming and expressing that they loved my talk, a little, thin man made his way through the crowd just to tell me that he was also a truck driver. It put him in the loop, so to speak, and gave him a connection to this week's speaker, which may have caused him to listen a little closer, maybe for the first time in a few weeks.

As I developed the ability to hear and obey God's voice as I prepared to speak and then gradually felt more comfortable in front of a large group of people, I noticed that people, especially in the back, would stretch their necks or position themselves to see me better. To me, this was an acknowledgment that I was doing a respectable job. In fact, one Sunday at another location, my wife, Mary, came with me, which she did not normally do. With me sitting in the front on the stand, a couple behind her in the congregation who did not know her were heard saying after looking at the program, "Oh, Brother Rioux is speaking today. I love his talks." Wow! I seemed to have come a long way from "Shut up, Jim" to this.

I also learned how not to introduce myself, which was to stop telling a story about how I would respond to people asking about my occupation. Week after week, an individual would approach me, and after asking me, I would tell them that I was a truck driver, to which they would always respond with an unexcited, even condescending reply of, "Oh!" I had to do something about this less-than-favorable response. So I started thinking that I could reinvent my description of being a truck driver that pulled a chemical tank and changed it to "a petrochemical relocation specialist." This sounded much more interesting, and the resulting reply of "Oh" had a decidedly more exciting ring to it. I told this story at the beginning of my talk, and while this was a completely true story, it was funny but not an appropriate one to precede a serious talk about spiritual matters. In fact, on one occasion, as I attempted to resume speaking, the laughter would also resume, so this story was dropped from my repertoire.

One should always begin speaking with an attention-grabbing line. Likewise, when writing, one should also begin with an interesting first line that will give a hint of the subject matter. I always told my children when preparing any type of paper for school to just write the first line, and God will fill in the rest. He has done so throughout my offerings on social media, with my published newspaper articles, and in this book. When we acknowledge God's presence in our lives and always do what is right in His sight, He will bless us with words.

We must also tell our own stories; telling the stories of others will diminish the audience's perception of their authenticity. Many years ago, the president of a university in the Western United States began a tradition of speaking to the student body at the beginning of each semester. He was an excellent speaker, with many delightful stories to connect to his subject matter. For a few semesters, he asked his wife to speak with him, which she refused. He persisted, and finally, she agreed to speak with him if he would write her talk. He agreed, but at the conclusion of the assembly, he found her backstage crying.

HIM. Darling, what is wrong?
HER. The talk you wrote for me was better than your own talk, but they loved your talk, and mine bombed. What happened?

His very eloquent response to his wife is what I want my family to always remember when writing or speaking.

HIM. Darling, the heart speaks to the heart.

We also began with Habakkuk from the Old Testament. He was a scribe who was called to be a witness to certain matters and then write about them for God's people. I have seen things that I thought I would never have the opportunity to speak or write about, but God knew. The four tables in this book had the recurring theme of God's exquisite timing and love. He placed me in the proximity of certain people and events at exact times. Again, they were interesting to me, but at the time, I did not understand why I was urged by the spirit to write about them on various platforms. God had prepared an audience to whom "He" wanted me to write for.

In the following stories, I do not know of any connective purposes other than He just wanted me to be a witness and then tell my family.

Many years ago, I was traveling north on Interstate 93 in New Hampshire when I started seeing signs that read, "Old Man Viewing

Ahead." As I came upon what looked like a small rest area, I could see people on a small rise, looking across the highway at a spot high up on the adjacent mountain. As I passed by, there was an obvious protrusion of rocks that gave the appearance of an old man's facial profile. *Oh*, I thought, *How cool that is*, and it was certainly a welcome surprise for a bored truck driver. Then, about a year later, in 2003, the rock formation collapsed after nature spent thousands of years forming it and was gone forever. Random? Yes. But God just wanted me to see it.

There are times when God will place us in a situation to simply experience certain feelings. This occurred on the same Canadian trip across the New Brunswick province that I mentioned in the introduction of this book. Since my entrance across the border in Maine, I have had goosebumps on my neck. Now I have seen many beautiful things throughout my trucking career that caused the same feelings, but only temporarily.

I traveled east along the coastal area of the Bay of Fundy, which lies between New Brunswick and Nova Scotia. I was listening to the public station, Radio One, all the way across the province as they were broadcasting strange, even spooky, maritime stories that would have accounted for some of the feelings I was having. But these feelings lasted all day, and until a few months later, I just did not have an explanation for my heightened senses, even the chills that traveled up and down my spine.

About six months later, I discovered the source of this unexplained feeling. My father's parents were Canadian immigrants who came as children to New York State and then settled in Massachusetts, where my father was born. I had begun to do family history work concerning my ancestral roots. As I was traveling across New Brunswick, unbeknownst to me, I was five hundred miles south of the St. Lawrence Seaway and the city of Trois-Pistoles, the port where a sixteen-year-old stowaway from Boulogne-sur-Mer, France, made his entrance into Canada in 1666. He was the first Riou(x) in my ancestral line to arrive in North America. I was in my family's native, ancestral homeland. This was the same type of experience that my wife was having concerning her deceased ancestors prior to her death. I was now having these same types of experiences as they were communicating through the spirit to me on this trip, one I will never forget.

In a circumstance closer to home in Baton Rouge, I was east-bound on the I-10 Mississippi River bridge. I was following a car carrier at the peak of the bridge that had just left a port terminal, which is a staging area for new cars that are offloaded from ships on the river. As I was following one of these trailers carrying Jeep Cherokees, the one on top in the back seemed to be bouncing more than usual. It concerned me enough that I changed lanes. I was thinking what a horrible thing it would be for it to bounce off that trailer. On the other side of the bridge, the truck and trailer went left at the split. I went right, and I forgot about it. That was until two mornings later, when I picked up the newspaper to see a story about a Jeep Cherokee that fell off the rear of an eastbound car carrier the day before on the top of the Mississippi River bridge, close to where I was two days earlier. God's exquisite timing, indeed, at least for me, not for the driver of that truck and trailer.

For many years of our marriage, Mary, who was from Goldsboro, North Carolina, tried to get me to try bar-b-q and slaw with a flair that was a regional favorite. I love pulled pork bar-b-q on a bun, and I love coleslaw, but not together in between the buns, snuggled up all against each other like they do in the Tar Heel state. She tried over and over to convert me but never succeeded. A couple of years after our marriage, with her at home in Louisiana, I had a delivery to make in Goldsboro, her hometown. Across the street from a fuel stop, I saw a little bar-b-q joint. I walked in, and the exchange I had with the lady behind the counter went something like this:

HER. Can I help you?
ME. Yes, ma'am. I will have some of your bar-b-q and slaw.

I then realized what I had just said and could hear Mary in my mind, telling me that in North Carolina, our slaw goes on the pulled pork. I then asked the lady.

ME. You *are* going to put that coleslaw off to the side, aren't you?

She then glared over the top of her glasses at me.

HER. You're not from here, are you?

I then look around only to find that all the patrons are looking at me as if I were an alien from a very distant planet.

ME. No, I'm not, ma'am, but I still want it on the side. Thank you.

Fast forward to late 2022, a year after Mary's death, I found myself in Jackson, Tennessee, the home of several roadside bar-b-q joints. I spied one next door to the truck stop and made a beeline for it. I was in heaven. I love these little, nondescript portable buildings that produce some of the best food in the area. I ordered two plates, one for now and one for supper that night. However, the one that I was getting was called "pulled pork bar-b-q on a bun" on the menu. I was so excited studying the menu, but when the guy asked if "I wanted that *with* slaw," I just said yes without thinking.

I walked back to the truck with both bags, each containing a separate meal. I then checked the bags. The chicken plate was in order; that was for supper, so I put it away. I then checked the pulled pork bag, only to find one item. "The dude forgot my coleslaw." I then could swear that I heard Mary's voice once again, reminding me that the slaw goes on the bun with the pulled pork. "Noooooooooooooo!" I screamed. I opened this huge foil-wrapped bun and found the coleslaw all in among my beautiful pulled pork.

Well, I thought to myself, *I am not going to bring it back*. It was my mistake. The only thing left to do was to eat it as much as I did not want to. And *then*, after twenty years of her pleading and cajoling, I thought, *Hey, this ain't bad. In fact, it's pretty good.*

At that point, I swear—I SWEAR—I could hear her laughing.

While I am telling stories about Jackson, Tennessee, my scariest trucking moment happened there in 2004, one that demonstrated God's love and intention to protect me. I was traveling west on I-40 as the sun was sinking in the sky, and it just began drizzling. I was behind a truck in the right lane that was in a contest of sorts with another truck in the left lane, with neither wanting to back down. This part of Tennessee is in the foothills of the Appalachian Mountains, and when two trucks are side by side, the heavier ones will slow down on an incline while the lighter ones will gain on the other. When the trucks reach the peak and begin the decline, the heavier ones will then gain on the lighter ones. These two were at it in front of me for about ten miles, with both being too stubborn to give way to the other.

As we were approaching an overpass, I could see a car moving slowly up the on-ramp with every intention of moving over in front of the truck ahead of me, so I backed off after having also done so earlier because of the rain.

However, the truck in the left lane decided, after 10 miles, to now jump in front of the truck directly in front of me at the same time as the car was about to merge in front of it. I saw all this happening and backed off even more.

As it was getting dark, the truck in front of me locked its brakes and was grinding to a complete stop. Even though I was more than a safe distance behind the truck in my lane, with wet pavement in conjunction with him unexpectedly stopping, I had no choice but to get on the shoulder with a very skinny gap to maneuver between the now-stopped truck and the concrete guard barrier.

In a series of events that seemed to occur in slow motion, I recalled barely threading that needle. I remember watching the back of my trailer clear the other trailer by less than a foot and seeing the hood of his truck in the open position because of the quick stop, breaking its restraining straps. I remember seeing the truck headlights shining down on the road.

Looking back, there was another problem after clearing the overpass. The truck that merged right at a most inopportune time decided to pull on the shoulder. Now I was faced with having to merge left quickly in front of the stopped truck in the right lane just as soon as I cleared it so that I did not rear-end the truck from the left lane that was now on the shoulder directly in front of me. By the grace of God, I watched the rear of my trailer barely miss the stopped truck in the right lane, just as I barely missed hitting the trailer on the shoulder. Nobody hit anyone, so I did not stop and did not know where the car from the on-ramp went.

I turned on my CB radio to ask if anybody hit anything, and after receiving an all-clear reply, one of the drivers told me that what he saw was an amazing bit of driving on my part. I thanked him but tried to put it out of my mind. About twenty miles later, I pulled into a rest area, thought about what had just happened, and realized that things could have ended very differently. I then started shaking uncontrollably for a few minutes. I realized that I had cheated death.

I give the glory to God, for He surely took the wheel.

As a concluding story to this "Afterthoughts" section and this book, there is an experience that I must relate to my grandchildren. I have struggled for months trying to decide whether to include it here in this book of stories. This one is of a sensitive nature, but one that I feel I must tell. For the reader, one must know that my beautiful grandchildren are of mixed race. Their fathers are African Americans. Previously, in my sixty-five years, I have not exactly been a stellar example of someone who has spoken of people of color in a Christlike manner. Each of us has hopefully grown as human beings and as true Christians as we have matured. I know I have.

After my first grandchild was born, I was placed on a fast track to accepting her as God gave her to us. In front of her father and his mother, I held her and stated that this little girl would teach all of us some life lessons. She has taught me the importance of family and getting together as often as the opportunity arises. She and her brothers have taught me perseverance through example and by challenging ourselves in difficult circumstances. For their valuable instruction, I am grateful.

In "First Table," I spoke of the two instances in which I was called for jury duty. In the second instance, I was in the first group selected to go through the process of either being selected or eliminated as potential jurors. Once in the courtroom, I was among the first group of fourteen who were called to sit in the jury box and referred to as juror 1.

Our first instruction was to be honest and unbiased as the questions were asked of each of us. Both the prosecuting and defense attorneys asked us if we could be completely unbiased. I responded as honestly as I could when I stated that I would do my best.

The defense attorney sort of scolded me as he restated that I am required to be totally unbiased. I responded as follows to the best of my recollection:

ME. Sir, there isn't a person in this room who is humanly capable of doing that. Everyone has a bias based on the life experiences that they brought here with them. Despite that, I will do my best, sir.

DEFENSE ATTORNEY. Can you be totally unbiased as you see the defendant sitting at the defense table with his attorneys?

ME. I know that with the initial crime scene team, forensics, and other evidence that was presented to detectives and then to the decision-makers in the various law enforcement agencies, and then to the district attorney, this young man has jumped through many proverbial hoops to be sitting where he is right now. He was not just chosen at random from off the street.

DEFENSE ATTORNEY. Juror 1, let me put it a little more bluntly to you. Can you be completely unbiased with this defendant who has a different skin color than you?

Madelyn, Lucas, Owen, Kenli, Camille, and Cannon, at that moment, each of your faces flashed before my eyes. I started to cry. This was visible enough that the bailiff brought me a box of tissue. I paused for a moment as I thought of each of you, and then I responded, now scolding the attorney.

ME. Sir, you do not know anything about me. If you did, you would know that I have six mixed raced grandchildren. We refer to them as our beautifully blended babies.

I paused again so that I could maintain my composure, and then I turned to the judge to ask him if I could pose a question to the defense attorney. Having been permitted to do so, I continued, but very briefly, as I turned back to address the attorney.

ME. Sir, as their grandfather, which race am I to teach them to hate?

Silence fell heavily over the courtroom, and then there was a noticeable gasp as everyone, including the judge, was now waiting for the defense attorney's reply.

DEFENSE ATTORNEY. No further questions for juror 1, Your Honor.

At that point, I was released.

There were so many purposes for which God placed me in that courthouse on two separate occasions, but I know that this exchange with this defense attorney was the most important reason so that my love for my grandchildren may be manifested publicly and that my impromptu emotional God-given reply might have instructed a few people present that day.

God will always place each of us among the right people, at the right time, for the right reason so that we may fulfill His purpose in us with our unique spiritual gifts.

Much love,
—Paw Paw

NOTHING IS RANDOM

These are God's stories that I had been called to witness and then write about. Each one of these stories, even the stories within a story, has threads of similar occurrences in the lives of the reader. I have often stated, "We are a sum of our life experiences," and the sum of similar experiences in the life of others creates a different but intriguing sum—a unique experience, a potentially fascinating story that is unique to their situation. Each of these is further evidence of God's exquisite timing and love whether we understand them immediately or years later.

There are eight billion people on this earth today, countless billions who belong to the eternities and an infinite number yet to be born. Imagining in my mind, all those stories past, present, and future that could potentially be written, reminds me of John 21:25:

> And there are also many other things which Jesus did, the which, if they should be written every one, I suppose that even the world itself could not contain the books that should be written. Amen.

God is in the details of each of our stories.

Nothing in our life is random—NOTHING!

Even with the messes of our life, God has prepared a message for us to tell.

To the readers, each of your stories must be told, or they just disappear, forever, like Charlie Fitts has instructed us in the "Preface."

As I am diligently striving to conclude this book, the stories continue to flood my mind. Having just mentioned the Charlie Fitts story from the movie *Taking Chance*, I'm reminded of a very recent spiritual prompting concerning the title of this book.

I was driving south on I-65 in Birmingham, Alabama, at about four in the morning. I was having second thoughts about the first title that I had come up with for this book. I felt that it would cause it to be shoved into a children's section in the bookstore. It certainly is appropriate for children but can and should be read by young and old. Out of nowhere, the current title manifested itself in my mind's eye. It stuck, and I'm pleased with the current title.

Just as quickly, another thought came to me. Again, an almost audible voice whispered to me, "Move Charlie Fitts to the front."

I was wondering, *What does this mean?* I then realized that the Charlie Fitts story, coupled with the importance of others telling their stories, would be excellent preface material to set the tone of this book.

But I hesitated as I maneuvered the truck on the ramp from I-65 to the I-59/20 split. I then moved to the left into the correct lane toward Tuscaloosa and then felt or heard the voice even more forcefully, even demanding me to "move Charlie Fitts to the front" because I had previously placed it here in this concluding section.

The feeling was so strong and felt right as I then got emotional. I knew that the change had to be made, and I'm glad I did.

So finally, in conclusion, write, speak, preach, dance, sing, build, and paint—it matters not.

If you have a feeling inside you that you just somehow know connects your life purpose with your spiritual gifts but can't seem to draw it out into the open, simply go back to the simplest verse in the Holy Bible for anyone with questions: "If any of you lack wisdom, let him ask of God" (James 1:5).

ACKNOWLEDGMENTS

I have so many people to thank, beginning with my daughters, Annie and Jessica, for their encouragement and for raising such beautifully awesome grand-young-ones. I thank Jessica for her courage to scream at me to get me to begin telling my stories. I am by no means finished with this task, for as long as I have breath, I will tell a story, whether anyone will listen or not.

I must acknowledge my brother Paul, who taught me many things during our long phone calls that ended only because one of our phones was dying or he had butterflies to milk, the encouragement beyond measure that he pours over me, giving me courage that I did not know existed and being the first to tell me of future books, something that was not on my radar. He told me he did not just mention it in passing; he knows.

To my friends on social media who have encouraged me with their many comments, *likes*, and *shares*; for the kind words of my friend in the funeral home; for all those Facebook friends in the Philippines and Africa, who by their presence, saw something in me that I didn't; for the little lady in the pharmacy who thanked me for my story about Wally.

I thank Mona, who will never know of the courage that she has instilled in me to just be myself.

To the critical family member who in his demeaning comments and criticism had, unbeknownst to him, issued a long-term challenge to me that I can now say as Nehemiah did in chapter 6, verses 2 and 3.

Sanaballat and Geshem sent unto me saying,
Come, let us meet together in one of the villages

in the plain of Ono. But they thought to do me mischief.

I am doing a great work, so that I cannot come down, why should the work cease, whilst I leave it and come down to you?

And I thank God for lifting the scales off my eyes and thus enabling me to see through spiritual eyes so that I may see all the connections between what He allows me to see and what He wants me to write. I am so grateful to be one of His scribes.

Much love, Madelyn, Lucas, Owen,
Kenli, Camille, and Cannon,
—Paw Paw
February 25, 2023

ABOUT THE AUTHOR

James, or Jim to his friends, was born to working-class parents as the fifth of nine children. He grew up in a north Baton Rouge, Louisiana, bedroom community and is currently a widower of three and grandfather to six. He was taught the value of a dollar through parental examples of frugal living, hence his desire to live a simple life.

As a truck driver for twenty-five years, with his retirement within his very short-term view, he hopes somehow to make up for years of watching the highway mile markers pass him by as his children grew up without his daily share of parental input. In dedicating this book to them and the many generations of children to follow, he hopes to impart to them the variety of stories that he has accumulated through the many miles and years, some of which he hasn't shared with anyone.

This book is not the conclusion of those untold stories but the beginning of his newly empowered gifts of storytelling through the written word. The recurring theme of God's exquisite timing has taught him that as he began to write, God's stamp of approval on each story caused him to become emotional and then do something very unexpected. As some of the details oozed up from an unknown source, he realized that some were revealed to him for the first time in an inexplicable manner. The reader is, therefore, encouraged to engage their own memory for stories about how this same spiritual occurrence might manifest itself. This gift is not exclusive to Jim.

Printed in the USA
CPSIA information can be obtained
at www.ICGtesting.com
LVHW051946240124
769470LV00086B/2352